P. Gordon Taylor

Charles Kingsford Smith

Ross & Keith Smith

Charles Ulm

GREAT STORIES OF AUSTRALIA

1. TO RIDE A FINE HORSE — Mary Durack
2. TREASURE FROM THE EARTH — Donald McLean
3. RIDERS TO AN UNKNOWN SEA — George Farwell
4. BY GRAVEL AND GUM — Nancy Keesing
5. PETER THE WHALER IN SOUTHERN SEAS — Max Colwell
6. TRAIL BLAZERS OF THE AIR — Kylie Tennant

Other titles in preparation

GREAT STORIES OF AUSTRALIA

GENERAL EDITOR: *Kylie Tennant*

TRAIL BLAZERS OF THE AIR

He edged along the strut.

TRAIL BLAZERS
OF THE AIR

by

KYLIE TENNANT

MACMILLAN
Melbourne • London • Toronto

ST MARTIN'S PRESS
New York

MACMILLAN AND COMPANY LIMITED
St Martin's Street, London WC2
also Bombay Calcutta Madras Melbourne

THE MACMILLAN COMPANY OF CANADA LIMITED
70 Bond Street Toronto 2

ST MARTIN'S PRESS INC
175 Fifth Avenue New York 10 NY

Library of Congress Catalog Card Number 66-13990

Registered in Australia for transmission by post as a book
PRINTED IN AUSTRALIA BY HALSTEAD PRESS, SYDNEY

To

CAPTAIN SIR P. GORDON TAYLOR, G.C., M.C.,

in admiration of his achievements

FOREWORD

A RICH YOUNG AUSTRALIAN, who had returned from a trip around the world, was asked by his friends what had impressed him most.

He was a fair boy, Peter, with his hair falling over his forehead, and always too long in the legs. He had a habit of sitting sprawled all over a chair instead of on it, and as he had made his way around the world by air, he must have been a trial to the air-hostesses, because even on the ground he couldn't stay still. When asked what had impressed him most, he sprang up and started to tramp to and fro, wearing a track in the carpet.

"The thing that impressed me most," Peter said, "was when the plane fell through the tarmac. We'd left Darwin for Sydney in this super new plane, the biggest and proudest and newest of them all. It was full of well-fed business men with briefcases, all looking very glossy and prosperous. White-coated stewards were wafting about bringing them champagne, and the business men were all busy impressing each other with their importance.

"The plane is purring along, and down below there is a sort of green-black fur of country with stretches of red, sandy dirt, but nobody in the plane takes any notice. Then, for some reason, the plane is diverted to this little airfield at the back of Queensland—don't ask me why— it was something important—and it comes roaring along the ground. There's a bump and it sinks down to its axles—too heavy, too big, too much altogether for this little airstrip. Now here is what is peculiar. All of a sudden everything went—the lights, the air-conditioning, the power. The stewards aren't bringing any more champagne. There's no food, nothing.

"The passengers are all clamouring at the crew wanting to know when they can fly on, and why isn't there any radio, and they'll miss their appointments. The captain looks as though he'll have a nervous breakdown. The crew look as though they're in mid-ocean with sharks. We had to sleep all night in the plane."

Peter laughed. "You should have seen those business men in the morning. All growing beards and looking like discontented pirates. They couldn't even shave."

At daylight, Peter, who was very much amused and interested to see what he called "the crumbling of civilisation", strolled away from the plane, walked two miles to a weather observatory on a hill, where he was given breakfast by a couple of men who told him that there would be a light plane flying in to take off passengers in a few hours. Then he went out and sat on the hill, looking down on the stranded and helpless plane where the passengers were still complaining and pestering the crew to do something. The flies were not too bad yet, although the rising sun told him it would be a day of fiery heat, over a hundred in the shade, if there was any shade.

"I thought," Peter said, "of what those early flyers did, repairing their planes with bits of fencing wire, carving out a new propeller from wood, finding a blacksmith somewhere who would forge a bit of metal for them.

"I thought of Bert Hinkler coming down alone in a place like this. He'd often sleep under the wing of his plane in the little rubber boat he carried in case he ditched into the sea. Besides he never had enough money for a hotel.

"I thought of the men who made Australian flying—going up and down from showgrounds, making a living by taking people for joyrides, so that they could scrape enough together for a new plane to take them on the flights around the world. Their little planes that brought

them from England to Australia, across the Pacific, all
those unheard-of flights that no one will ever do again—
their planes would fit into the baggage compartment
of this monster.

"They didn't have *anything*. They just relied on themselves. And I looked at that passenger plane, that huge,
beautiful, civilised plane; and I laughed."

When Peter got back to the airfield, an old woman had
arrived from somewhere in the scrub and was boil-
ing tea in a blackened kerosene tin over a fire. The dirty
and thirsty passengers stood about, looking in horror at
this empty, bare country where the sky came down to
your boots. For many of them this was their first experience of Australia, and they couldn't get back to the city
quick enough. But Peter was quite at home. He knew that
from little strips of bare ground in the bush had soared
up a whole generation of airmen. As children, they had
once waited in lonely places to see Hinkler or Kingsford
Smith or Parer and McIntosh fly in. They had been
too poor to go up; but sometimes the worshipped, the
wonderful hero, had taken up the kids for nothing.

"It's the kids with the autograph books," Kingsford
Smith had said. "The bush kids."

Being famous in Australia did not mean riches or the
regard of great men. It meant being worshipped by the
small boys who would one day be pilots themselves,
just because they had once seen an airman or had a
word with him.

No country in the world needed the planes and the
men to fly them more than the huge, hard country where
civilisation was just a distant city on the coast. No
country bred greater flyers, or saw them do greater deeds.

"You should have seen those passengers rush the relief
plane when it came in," Peter said. "They wanted *out*—
away from the heat and the flies and the emptiness and

the feeling that nobody was going to do anything for them, no matter how much money they had. You don't feel important in country like that."

Peter stayed on with the crew. He wasn't in a hurry. They had the radio repaired; they were getting men together to repair the plane, a tractor came bustling up and competently the work of getting the great plane airborne began. It was all teamwork. Next time there would be a wider, longer airstrip that would bear the plane's weight. There would be bigger and bigger planes.

But the men who had first made it possible were ghosts riding the red dust-storms and the lightning of the sky. The dawn and sunset of their day glowed still above the clouds and the far-off cities. Bravery is not lost, and the faint exhaust-plume of the Trail Blazers had just passed over the horizon of time.

"It impressed me," Peter said. "Nothing I saw all the way around the world impressed me like that."

CONTENTS

CHAPTER		PAGE
	Foreword	ix
One	You have to die some time. This may be it	1
Two	Warmest congratulations	10
Three	You are safe in the air. But you have to come down to the ground	22
Four	To share in everything	29
Five	The bubble reputation	41
Six	A man's plane is like his horse	47
Seven	A storm is full of bumps	57
Eight	Fame is a magnet for disaster	63
Nine	An airline is supposed to make money	74
Ten	The Australia-England run	84
Eleven	The flame from the exhaust	92
Twelve	To be a hero is not enough	100
Thirteen	A man is safe with the stars for friends	104
Fourteen	About a thousand miles. A little out of gliding distance from land	114
	The trails they blazed	123
	Editor's notes	129

Chapter One

YOU HAVE TO DIE SOME TIME. THIS MAY BE IT

WIZARD STONE looked at the crowd in the dirty little tent with a cold eye, the eye of a circus lion. These "hicks", as he privately called them, had paid to see the plane; he had given his speech about it.

"And that will be all, ladies and gentlemen. Please pass out. The show is closing for the night."

It was 1912, and here he was in a little Queensland sugar town, Bundaberg, with the same crowd he had known in America, men in shirt-sleeves, women in light frocks, pushing in to exclaim at the strange contraption like a great insect that smelt of metal and castor oil.

"When you going to fly it?"

"Oh my!" a girl giggled. "Fancy going up in *that!*"

They were not really impressed by the frail plane or the little man beside it. Maybe he had managed to fly the thing five hundred and four miles in France, and even soar over Sydney. Maybe he had survived a dozen smashes. It was billed as a Bleriot, built to the same plan as that of the man who, four years before, had asked, "Where is Dover?" and set off across the Channel without compass or chart.

But that didn't prove anything. It was just a stunt.

"*If* it goes up . . ." a beefy young Queenslander said loudly. "Which it won't."

"Pass out please," Wizard Stone demanded. "Owing

to circumstances beyond our control the flight will not take place."

He noticed, when they had all gone, that there was still one young man left. "Out, son," he said firmly. "You've seen it."

"Mr Stone," the young man stammered, "I know why your plane won't fly. I can fix it, Mr Stone."

"So you can fix it? Ever seen a plane before?"

"No, but I've worked in the foundry," the young man offered hopefully. "And I took a correspondence course in aviation. And look!" He fumbled out a school exercise book, full of newspaper cuttings and blurred photographs. This was the local Boy Wonder, Stone thought sarcastically. There he was in the photographs with a team of other boys pushing his home-made glider off the sandhills of the beach.

A home-made glider on the sandhills.

"It's the top wires," the young man said. "The top wing wires need to be as strong as those underneath. I read about it in *Flight*, Mr Stone."

Stone looked at the kid's hands. His face with the wide-spaced eyes that meant courage; the small strong body didn't tell him as much as those hands with the chips out that meant using tools, and the thumbs set almost independent of the hands, a sign that indicates the stubborn and lonely creator.

"Show me," Stone said. The boy moved his hands over the wing of the plane. When he was talking about what he knew, his nervousness fell away. He was sure and, Stone realised suddenly, he was right. Nineteen years old, the Boy Wonder knew about planes.

The top wires need strengthening.

"I can fix the carburettor," he offered. "I listened to the engine, and it needs tuning."

While he talked, A. B. Stone watched him. There's one in every town, he thought. They know all about Lawrence Hargrave, still alive in Sydney, "the mad kite flyer", the brilliant engineer-astronomer, who had studied lift and stability and the behaviour of air with box-kites along the Sydney beaches. It was Lawrence Hargrave who had invented the first rotary engine, whose discoveries, sent all over the world in scientific papers, quickened other men's minds thousands of miles away. The Germans had his models in a special building in the Munich Museum. Ideas, the Australian inventor said, should be free. In Munich, students and engineers from all over Europe could see his models.

These youngsters like the Boy Wonder joined the Aerial League, founded by George Taylor, friend and co-experimenter with Hargrave who took the chair at the first meeting. "What is Australia doing?" Taylor would demand in print. "Last year, China opened a school for aviators. In three weeks, ten aviators were trained—and they were good aviators, too. Why can't we do better?" Or "Japan has four captains and twenty-four lieutenants undergoing aeronautical instruction in Germany. There is no doubt Germany is fighting hard for command of the air." "Australia pleads for an aerial fleet. The airship as the democrat of warfare will lift the least populated nation to a level with the greatest."

Urged by Taylor, who belonged to the Army Intelligence Corps, the Commonwealth Government had in 1909 offered a prize of £5,000 for an Australian-built aeroplane flown by an Australian. Young men in gliders began falling out of the air all over the country.

It was Taylor's Aerial League which invited Harry Houdini, the famous escapologist, to make what must be regarded as the first real powered flight in Australia. Houdini brought his own Voison plane for the tour, and Hargrave had the wry experience of seeing what were really his box-kites writ large into the French plane—without, of course, any acknowledgement from the makers.

"Son," Wizard Stone said, studying the Boy Wonder, "sit down and we will talk about flying." The young man eagerly accepted the invitation. "Some kids catch it early and get over it. Yours seems to be a chronic case. I remember now seeing you here before with your family. A nice family, if I may say so. Mother, little brother and sisters; and you're earning good money at the sugar mill, I guess?"

The young man flushed. "I could talk Mum round."

"Yeah, you could talk Mum round. Now, an aeroplane is just a freak thing that people pay to see. Some guy builds a plane from pictures he's seen, adding little touches of his own. There's this boy Duigan, out in your Victorian scrub, that used piano wires to build his plane and steel straps off his father's wool bales. He had a motor bike engine, so all he has to do is turn it into an aero engine, by hand. The radiator he solders by hand—500 fins. He carves the propeller from local wood. And the durn thing flew!"

"If my father was a squatter," Stone's visitor sighed, "I'd be going to England like Duigan to learn to fly properly."

"Sure, you would! And when you've learnt it, what is there in it? You get a booking at country fairs. You might even have a manager, and let me tell you, they're all unreformed burglars. The field is too small to fly out of, and the crowd yells for your blood. The wind blows like hell, the motor packs up. You tell them you'll fly if they cut down those trees. They call you a quitter and threaten to smash you and the plane. Ask them to go up with you, and there's no takers. So you use a lot of bad language and they go away. That's flying!" His cold eye lit up. "But, oh boy! it's not just the loops and flipflops and the upturned faces. I've seen the greatest of them all going round a half-mile track, just flicking the dust with his wingtips on the turns. He had a magnificent funeral. Magnificent! Used to go up with fireworks spurting all over the plane, and come down in time to put it out when it caught fire. One night he didn't.

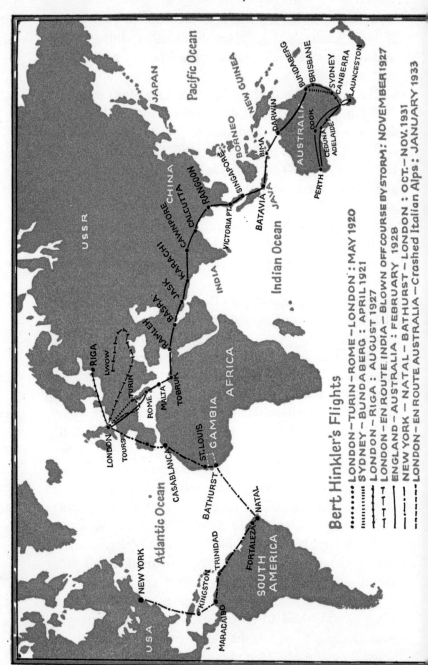

Bert Hinkler's Flights

••••••• LONDON–TURIN–ROME–LONDON : MAY 1920
|||||||| SYDNEY – BUNDABERG : APRIL 1921
•–•–•– LONDON – RIGA : AUGUST 1927
↑↑↑↑↑ LONDON–EN ROUTE INDIA – BLOWN OFF COURSE BY STORM: NOVEMBER 1927
———— ENGLAND – AUSTRALIA : FEBRUARY 1928
–––––– NEW YORK – NATAL – BATHURST – LONDON : OCT.– NOV. 1931
–··–··– LONDON–EN ROUTE AUSTRALIA –Crashed Italian Alps : JANUARY 1933

"Maybe you get sued for busting the grandstand, or if you're lucky you miss it by an eyelash, and disappoint them all. Son, you get to *despise* people who come to see you die. Sure, the plane holds together because the engine and the tail have a sentimental fancy for each other. But what they're waiting for out there," he hooked his thumb at the tent door, "is not to see you succeed, but to see you carried off in three pieces. Shall I tell you what makes an aviator? Just to be able to walk away from the plane when it hits the ground. Get over it now before it's too late."

"I'm going to Brisbane," the boy said. "To show my glider at the Exhibition. I can get a plumber's job in the Water and Sewerage Board."

"You'll eat better that way. I, myself," Stone said thoughtfully, "will be going back to Brisbane. Come round tomorrow early, and let's see what you can do with those struts. I could do with a mechanic—a good one. If you're any good, I'll see you back in Brisbane. By the way—what's your name?"

"Bert, Mr Stone, I'm Bert Hinkler. I'll be here tomorrow. And I'll be waiting in Brisbane."

It was not until they reached New Zealand that Bert Hinkler recovered from the pure joy and amazement that he was in partnership with the "Wizard", bad as the little man's luck seemed to be. It had relented sufficiently to find him a backer for the New Zealand tour, but in Auckland, for all Bert's frantic efforts with the engine, it looked as though the Wizard would not be airborne. And for once they had perfect weather, with people thickening the grandstands like flies.

"She'd better move, son," Stone murmured. "There's 30,000 out there, and all the great white chiefs of the islands among them."

"What's keeping you, Stone?" his backer called.

"They've been waiting over an hour and a half."

"Our boy Bert is fixing it," Stone said cynically. "The Boy Wonder has it in hand."

His helper lifted a perspiring and grease-streaked face from the engine. "That's about it," he said. With some foreboding he helped wheel the machine from the tent.

It was greeted with a roar. The motor coughed tetchily and then roared back. Bert breathed again. The Bleriot was unpredictable. Sometimes she flew, sometimes she didn't. There was Stone taxi-ing down the course. He was in the air. Then the Bleriot seemed to be fighting for her own way. Over the fence she swooped; had she cleared it? No. She had hit the hill on the other side of the fence.

There was another shout as the crowd came swarming out, men running to the crash. At least Stone was alive because he seemed to be trying to murder the foremost rescuers, but in spite of him those large and excited New Zealanders moved like meat-ants on the plane. Before Bert's eyes, encouraging each other, they had picked the wounded plane up, holding the sagging tail, and man-handling it to the fence, dropped it over. Then, coming up with a run, hundreds of hands tugging, the plane was carried shoulder-high to the tent.

But the confused goodwill was turning to hostility. "Go on up! Get her into the air! Give us our money back!"

Stone limped in and closed the tent door. "Ah well," he said philosophically, "let's see what our helpers have done in the way of damage."

But time passed, and outside the mounted police were put to it, charging that part of the crowd which showed signs of tearing down the tent. One of the horses tangled in a tent rope and fell down.

"Even the horse," Stone croaked, "has caught the falling sickness."

The inspector of police burst into the tent, showing signs of struggle. "You men get out of here," he shouted, "before they wreck the joint. We can't hold them."

The Wizard took no notice. He and Bert were busy seeing what could be done to the Bleriot. It was another hour or so before the last angry spectators left, shouting abuse.

"Like I told you, son," Stone said. "You got to be able to walk away from the plane."

"It'll pick up," Bert said confidently. "We can rebuild her."

And it did pick up, with the rebuilt plane really flying; and the New Zealanders so friendly that it was a good thing Bert slept in the tent, where he could prevent them from taking some little souvenir like a piece of the wing fabric or a chip out of the propeller.

Bert Hinkler wrote to his mother that he was not doing anything dangerous like flying. They were working up a stunt where a racing car on the ground tried to beat the plane in the air. On a trial run, Bert was just sitting in the car with a stop watch, timing, while the driver tried to see how fast he could take the curves.

When a tyre blew out and the car crashed, Bert's arm was nearly severed at the shoulder. The doctors thought they might have to amputate, but luckily did not. He was away from work in hospital for some weeks. And when he came back, there was a final misfortune; the plane crashed and the Wizard broke his collarbone. True, he walked away, shaky, but still on his feet.

The tour was over, and it had lost about £600, with both the plane and the aviator out of action for the time being.

"Just another place that will ache when the weather changes," Stone observed.

Chapter Two

WARMEST CONGRATULATIONS

At PENRITH, near Sydney, there was a flying school run by Bill Hart who held the first pilot's licence in Australia. Bert Hinkler worked for him until he turned twenty-one and could go to England to break into real aircraft. All his life he dreamed of someone backing him in building a new type of aeroplane which his practical experience convinced him would be a leap ahead of those he patched together.

With a friend he worked his way to Europe on a German freighter, and found that the £75 fee at the London Flying School was beyond his means. But he was soon working at the Sopwith factory, mainly because it was so difficult to stop him, and here with new designs, and new aircraft, he was really at the centre of activity. As soon as war broke out in 1914 he was accepted by the Royal Naval Air Service. Five foot three and a half inches, eyes grey, complexion dark, and his trade was "aeroplane erector".

As "observer", he found himself in 1915 going up, armed; an old rifle loaded with incendiary bullets against a bombing Zeppelin, which luckily went away. After eighteen months' training he was writing home enthusiastically that his family would be "absolutely astounded at what aeroplanes are able to do today". He invented a "little attachment" for bomb-dropping gear. Later it was a double machine gun; he was always inventing.

As a gunner in a fighter squadron based on Dunkirk,

he came to dread the cold. Huddled in the rear cockpit, with a Lewis gun that was very poor compared with the German forward-firing guns, he had to take off his fur gloves and load with his bare hands in sub-zero weather. He made a hundred and twenty-two flights over enemy territory, including night bombing raids, and was awarded

An old rifle against a Zeppelin.

the D.S.M. In the autumn of 1917 he was on leave wangling to graduate into the newly formed Royal Air Force. He was also about to marry a hospital sister, Nancy, who at that time possibly thought that being a pilot's wife would be wonderful.

He became a qualified pilot in time to be sent to the Italian front—hard, gruelling flying against the retreating Austrian army—and then the war was over. He had a crazy dream that had been with him for a long time. He was going to fly home to Australia, alone, to "Bundy". He had always been quiet, methodical, an inventor. Now he wanted a plane that was light but with large fuel tanks. He had his war pay and his connection with Sopwith's, but nobody would back him with the really big money needed for such a flight.

Like every other Australian airman in England, he was

eager to enter for the great England-Australia race and win the £10,000 that had been offered by the Commonwealth Government for the first flight from England to Darwin within thirty days. But he knew also in his heart that Ross Macpherson Smith who had spent his war service in the Middle East and knew the conditions and what landing grounds there were, had an overwhelming advantage. Ross Smith deserved to win.

So Hinkler continued as a test pilot, one of the few civilian test pilots in the business. When something went wrong, he could land his plane so skilfully that he did not damage the aircraft. Then he would walk back to the hangar and later find out what caused the fault.

He took off for Australia.

By late 1919 he had a "pretty battered" Baby Avro that he had saved to buy. He wanted a plane that he could service himself, and to which he could fit the large fuel tanks which made the difference in long-distance flying. One cold morning in May 1920 he quietly took off for Australia and although he created a new record for long-distance, non-stop flight in a light plane, he was bitterly disappointed to be stopped by a little local war in Syria, and hostilities in Egypt. There was no official reception on his return to the Avro field at Hamble. He just pushed the plane into the hangar and took his motor bike and rode home.

The following year he sailed for Australia with the Baby Avro in the ship's hold, and from Sydney he flew it to Bundaberg. He was not thinking of the two world records he had broken by doing so. He just took two apples and a slice of apple pie with him, and set off causing, of course, tremendous excitement and local pride when he put the Avro down in the paddock next to his father's

The Avro down in the paddock.

house with the same lack of fuss that he would have wheeled in a bicycle.

There was something he had to do—not just for himself. He remembered Wizard Stone and the broken-down little Bleriot that flew sometimes when it was in the mood. Now he looped and spiralled and rolled about the sky over Bundaberg, the Baby Avro ducking under bridges, roaring and dancing in the air, skimming the river, soaring over the people, the "kids" that came running, faces upturned, following him as he rode the plane along the roadway, taxi-ing back to his father's house from flights to little towns that had never seen a plane. The notables gave him cheques, and they were welcome; his town gave him worship; and then—for he

had broken records—in the big cities, people began to talk
of him. But—shadow of Wizard Stone's luck—his Baby
Avro was blown out of shape when he landed in a gale
on a beach on his way back to Sydney. Sadly, towed by
farm horses for fifteen miles, the plane made a funereal
journey, Hinkler driving the horses to a place where he
could hire a truck and convey the remains to the city
to be patched up and sold.

Sadly towed by farm horses.

There were no jobs in Australia and he had his job in
England. He would have to go back on the small sums
given him by the little towns. He was just a test pilot
again; a shy, quiet man who climbed into the plane wearing a bowler hat as if to show he was not one of the flashing
and dashing officer types. He was cautious, careful to the
point of fussiness. Everything had to be exactly right,
perfect. But when he was flying for a prize, always alone,
his light planes did hair-raising things.

He needed prize money. He still had to make that flight
to Australia. During a King's Cup Race he and another
competitor landed in the fog together at opposite ends of
the field, missing each other by a few feet. By 1927 he
was testing his light plane, the Avro Avian, on a non-stop
flight to Riga, making a new world record. He still could

not find the money or the backers for the flight to Australia. Too many men had died on long-distance flights.
The same look was on the faces of rich men that he had
seen in the crowds around the grubby tent of the Bleriot.
He would have to make the trip on his own savings. He
was married now, but Nancy, his wife, knew what this
meant to him.

When he set off in February 1928, he was thirty-five. In
Rome he had trouble with the language, worry about
landing his plane amid tall, unseen wireless masts on the
wrong airfield. The R.A.F. men in Malta nearly killed
him with forceful hospitality. He missed Tobruk and
landed in sand, spending the night under the wing of his
plane in his little rubber raft. Headwinds and Arabs,

Sleeping under the wing in a rubber raft.

delays in workshop overhauls of the engine, the medical
clearance in Palestine; all the buzzing worries of the
ground sank away in the cramped monotony and roar of
flight.

Such a small plane! He was being commended in print
as he forged on across the world. But, of course, the
plane would crash. Little planes did crash; so many had.
At Jask, in Persia, he found the petrol leaking. At this
primitive stop there were no means to make repairs.
Perhaps he could forge on to Karachi before the petrol

all leaked away? It was a nerve-racking flight. The petrol was fed from tank to tank, and he had reserves. That petrol leak hurried him along to a new record. He put his tropical solar topee on to protect his head from the sun. It did not protect his ears from the roar or his red-rimmed eyes from the strain.

In the cities, newspapers which had said that little planes crashing discouraged aviation, now told their readers that little private planes like Hinkler's, if they succeeded, must do aviation harm, because other men would try to do what he was doing and fail.

Meanwhile, in his oil-stained overalls, Hinkler would probe the plane, listening and tightening and tuning. However exhausted he might be when he came down, he tended the plane first. At Singapore, the weight of the petrol sank the wheels into the mud. It was pouring rain. Pushed by the crowd, he ploughed and staggered off. They heaved him just as the boys had done when he flew his glider in the Bundaberg sandhills. There was goodwill from the crowd of little foreign men. He was in the air over Java, fourteen days from London; and the record was twenty-eight days. Nine hundred miles to Darwin, and the storm-torn terrible weariness of the flight almost behind him.

In Australia, people were saying that they knew he could do it. A tired, small chap, not very impressive, in a double-breasted suit who had flown just on 11,000 miles, alone, in fifteen and a half days. His wife heard in London from the press representatives that he was there. Now she might breathe again, sleep again, without the weight of foreboding.

Hinkler was a hard man to lionise. He had offers for lecture tours—which he did not accept, being no talking man. Would he be offered a knighthood? He was driven in flag-draped cars through cheering streets. At the capital, he kept His Majesty's representatives waiting in the rain, while he carefully wrapped the tarpaulin over his plane. He made speeches, good, sensible, modest speeches. He wanted to get it into their heads that flying was safe and useful. Not a stunt, nothing flashy. He was presented with gifts.

His knighthood was made a political battle. Was it not given just because he was a workman's son, the newspapers demanded? From London came a royal message of "warmest congratulations" and the award of the Air Force Cross to Lieutenant Hinkler.

"But I'm not even a Boy Scout!" Hinkler said in bewilderment. What did he want with a military medal? He was a civilian, flying a plane that was his own property. Laboriously trying to do its best, the Commonwealth Government made him an honorary squadron leader of the Royal Australian Air Force. Hinkler never used the title. He was tired of well-meaning, pompous people, brass hats, important guests at receptions. Someone tried to sabotage his plane, blocking a pipe with waste before he left for Tasmania. Was it one of those who just didn't like to do without the crash for which the crowd paid?

He removed the plug of waste that had been deliberately pushed into the oil pipe. In June, he was back in Bundaberg again, his round-Australia tour over. He had done everything he had said he would. On his thirty-sixth birthday he was back in England with a little company and a factory to produce an amphibian plane of his own design. The money had come from his Australian windfall. But the depression closed in, and no firm would take up his plane. He tried in America to interest business men in his Ibis as an ideal plane, easy to use for private flying. If business men had no money for a private plane, it could be hired. At thirty-nine, he was an inventor, a designer, a battler for civilian flying, with years of hard work and lack of encouragement behind him. He needed money badly.

Well, if he had to stunt, he would do so. But he made no resounding announcement in advance. Perhaps, he thought, if he pulled off a great flight, some firm might take up his Ibis plane. Maybe someone would back him. It was Wizard Stone again on the grand scale. All over the world, in 1931, aviators were racing each other for records. Hinkler had a wonderful skill in navigation and in handling a plane. He knew he was among the best, but he was not a showman.

Now he left New York and very few people knew where he was going. He had methodically planned his movements, flying non-stop from New York to Jamaica in eighteen hours: a new record, the first non-stop flight over the route. Then, a week later, he soared off across the seven hundred miles of the Caribbean Sea to Maracaibo in Venezuela, using his uncanny skill to navigate zig-zag past storms. His next stop was Trinidad, then Paramaribo in Dutch Guiana, and on along the north-east coast of Brazil. He was, he said cagily, "just touring around". He was having trouble with hot-tempered officials who demanded his visa and did not speak English; but, after the usual set-to, the intervention of a British Consul and a good deal of shoulder-shrugging and hand-waving, he was in Natal—the Brazilian Natal on the far eastern tip of South America.

This was to be his taking-off point for the flight he had planned: the first flight ever made over the South Atlantic to Africa. He expected bad weather over that ocean, and he met it. He flew in a blue flame of lightning in immediate danger of death with the roar of the motor as his only companion. The Atlantic gale never let up; and neither did the dogged man in the little plane. He carried no radio, and no one would ever know what happened to him if the storm won. By morning he was in clear air with a toy steamer below him in the blue sea, and he swooped down exultantly to greet it.

At seven o'clock, punctual as a milk delivery, he had arrived only ten miles south of Bathurst, in Gambia, West Africa, where he planned to land. His flight had set three new records but he sent his wife a laconic telegram: "Landed at Bathurst, Gambia. O.K. Bert."

Bad weather over the ocean.

By easy stages he made his way via Casablanca and Madrid to England to be carried shoulder-high from the plane. There was the crowd which always cheered if you succeeded, the reception with champagne and sandwiches, the telegrams. There was the Minister for Air apologising for the absence of the Prime Minister, the representative from Australia House apologising for the absence of the High Commissioner. But did anyone offer to back his plane or help him find some chance to use his brains and skill? They did not. He was on his own, as he always had been. The Ibis gathered dust in the barn beside his house, so ironically called Mon Repos.

Hinkler was quieter than ever about his plans. If he had to go on stunting, the Australians had the most generous crowds. He would go home. In his usual way he set off

C

without making any press noise about it. He telephoned a couple of friends to see him off, and they waited in the fog until it lifted in the early hours of one raw January morning, 1933. He was going home to "Bundy" and the crude, good-humoured, generous people who were his own kind.

The powerful engine beat faithfully as the plane rose in the mist. Nobody worried about Bert Hinkler because he never took chances. He was so expert, so completely master of himself, his fate and his aircraft. Nobody made any enquiries because he had always turned up before. When he did not, the governments of France, Switzerland and Italy sent out search parties. The rumours grew. His body was not found until spring when the snow melted on the high Apennines of Italy.

The Italian Government lavished on Hinkler's funeral all the solemn ostentation, the full military honours that the warm-hearted people wished. There were flags and flowers all the way to Florence where his body lay in state at the Aero Club, guarded by Italian soldiers and airmen while crowds filed past. In the evening, with aeroplanes soaring overhead and the muted music of military bands, the funeral procession moved slowly through the streets.

On the mountain where he had crashed a great monument was erected through the efforts of the local flying club. In the last war it was destroyed by trigger-happy partisans. Hinkler's better memorial, the Ibis plane, was left in the barn at Mon Repos for twenty years. Efforts to bring it to Australia were ignored. It was exhibited at a garden party and then demolished. His inventions were either quietly appropriated or passed over.

But none of that could matter now to the proud, casual man. He had been lying, when they found him, in a little hollow, with his helmet off, settled down waiting for the storm to pass or a break in the luck when he could go off to repair the plane. He was badly hurt when he climbed out of the plane into the snowstorm, more badly than he realised. He was dying. But he walked away from the plane.

Chapter Three

YOU ARE SAFE IN THE AIR, BUT YOU HAVE TO COME DOWN TO THE GROUND

POINT COOK, on the western shore of Port Phillip Bay, has for more than half a century been the mother base of the Royal Australian Air Force. But the four young pilots who began flying there in the first month of the war of 1914 flew only at dawn and sunset, when there was no wind.

They left behind a legend that they regularly crashed their planes on Friday afternoons so they could get week-end leave. Many years later "Tommy White", when he was Sir Thomas White, Minister for Aviation, would recall that one of the buildings bore a large dint he had made in it with his Bristol box-kite.

"We flew by sensation," he explained, "because we had no instruments except a barometer. There was no enclosing fuselage and no floor. We kept check on the engine with our ears and the rush of air in the face told us whether the climb or glide was at the right angle."

In 1911 the Minister for Defence had returned from an Imperial Conference brimming over with the idea of a Central Flying School. This would provide a daring breed of birdmen who would ring the coasts with air power. All such happy predictions were a little premature because in the first place there were no landing grounds, and in the second many years were to elapse before aviation in Australia emerged from the most desperate kind of muddle. Point Cook had its critics even in 1911 when a young man, Harry Hawker, later famous for the Hawker "Hurricane", sneered at the limping Deperdussin monoplanes and the Bristol box-kites, their canvas fabric rotted coming by boat through the tropics. Hawker demanded hydroplanes for a coast watching force around Australia.

Point Cook was ready to train its first four pilots in 1914 only because Henry Petre and Eric Harrison laboured like fiends in rain and mud to produce an aerodrome of a primitive sort with canvas hangars and the poor planes, little more than gliders. One of the first student pilots was Captain Richard Williams who, by the time he was thirty-one, was Chief of Staff of the R.A.A.F., the first Australian Air Marshal, and for many years Director-General of Civil Aviation.

In February 1915 the Government of India sent a desperate message: Had Australia any airmen, mechanics or planes for the war in Mesopotamia? The Australian Government replied that it could send its four trained pilots, it could send mechanics. Aeroplanes? No, unfortunately; no planes. The mechanics, most of whom had never seen a plane, were rushed through a course at Point Cook, and two trucks were equipped as repair shops.

The First Half-Flight of the Australian Flying Corps, in its parade photograph, resembles a gathering of unemployed pirates. Only the officers had uniforms until a day or so before sailing. One of the more piratical-looking was later Air Vice-Marshal G. Mackinolty, Air Vice-Marshal and member of the Australian Air Board.

The planes they had to fly in Mesopotamia were what could be "spared" from other theatres of war, and a two-pound bomb to be thrown by hand was the usual horror weapon. For convenience, holes were cut in the floor of the cockpit so that the bomb could be pushed out. If there was any wind, it was a great comfort to the pilot to know that his plane could fly backwards; and the local wind, the *shamal*, in a temperature of 105° in the shade, was a dust-laden hell, blowing down tent-hangars and splitting them to ribbons. Sunstroke was common.

On one occasion Thomas White and his observer taxied along the ground for fifteen miles to safety when their machine would not lift them into the air. The only way across the sandhills was by a road which lay close to a Turkish position. The observer stood up with his rifle to direct the course and beat off attack while White drove

Beating off attacks with a rifle.

past the Turks. With an instrument that resembled a small garden rake White, holding it to eye level, would map out an enemy position by the degrees of distance from the pegs to the centre. He and his observer, Captain Yeats-Brown of the Indian Army, were eventually taken prisoners by the Turks and spent much of the war in an underground cell in Constantinople, until they escaped to Bulgaria.

Wounded, dead, or prisoners-of-war, the Australian airmen fought a fierce war in Mesopotamia, Palestine and from Egypt. Australia was the only Commonwealth country to maintain its own air force.

Flying in Australia was entirely a military matter by 1919. The public was further assured that flying was not for them when the Commonwealth Government decided to raise some money for a peace loan and sent ex-Air Force flyers around the country selling bonds. It was a wonderful way of disposing of old army planes, and one spectacular crash after another conveyed the news that the cow-paddock landing grounds were not really fit to land on.

Nevertheless, pilots returned from the war were pooling their pay to buy leftover planes. Little mushroom companies enticed the more reckless citizens to pay for the risk of going up from country showgrounds.

The real blaze of enthusiasm for air-faring sprang up over the air race to Australia, with its prize of £10,000 for any Australian or group of Australians to fly first from England to Darwin within thirty days. Thanks to the war, the map now boasted aerodromes where planes could land, refuel and take off on a route to Australia. Some of these aerodromes were little more than flat places with a shed and a few drums of aviation spirit, but they were there.

Ross Macpherson Smith, who had transferred from the Australian Light Horse to the Flying Corps, knew those little dromes from Egypt through to India. He had been pilot to Lawrence of Arabia and was first among the Allied Air Force to fly over Jerusalem. By the end of the war he had collected three Distinguished Flying Crosses and two Military Crosses. He had flown two generals in what was considered a giant plane from Cairo to Calcutta; and two of his comrades, Shiers and Bennett, had gone with him on the flight. He had been on a further mission by sea to spot out possible landing grounds through the Indies to Timor.

The Vickers-Vimy firm was ready to back him with a plane, and it only remained to gather in his brother,

Keith, to complete the party. But it was a grim battle before Ross and Keith Smith could arrive in a blaze of glory. After leaving England they did not find any good weather until they reached Basra, the old aerodrome in Mesopotamia that the Australians had improvised in the war. They ran into snow clouds over the French coast. Ice coated their face masks; their sandwiches were frozen solid. Cramped in the small, open cockpit, with cloud, snow and blinding rain, they tried flying over or under the storms. It took them five days to reach Taranto in Italy, and another five to Basra. By that time they were tired out, and their plane needed overhauling. They were relieved by the good behaviour of the Vickers-Vimy over India and took heart to press on faster as they made Calcutta and then Rangoon.

The Siamese version of a good aerodrome at Singora nearly finished them. "A square patch had been hewn from the jungle," wrote Ross Smith, "the trunks and upper portions of the trees had been removed, but the stumps were allowed to remain. We made a safe but miraculous landing, missing the stumps by inches." Pouring rain was no help.

At Singapore, the racecourse was "suitable though small"; but a foreboding warned Ross Smith that he was approaching most hazardous landing grounds. His spirits rose again when he learned that the Governor-General of the Dutch East Indies (now Indonesia) had had aerodromes especially constructed for the aeroplanes flying from England to Australia.

At Sourabaya, they found that the landing ground, with its shining, hard surface, had been laid over an unreclaimed swamp into which the Vickers-Vimy sank dismally to the axles. Time was running out, and they thought they would never get off the ground. Out of the bog the machine crawled on to a roadway of mats contributed by the villagers, a runway of bamboo 350 yards long. Swarms of little men panted and pushed the plane on this frail path, and in a shower of bamboo splinters the flyers took off.

Now they were so tense that they could not sleep. They overhauled the plane for the sea jump to Darwin. Hours rolled by with the blue water of the Timor Sea below; and pilots of those days were nervous as cats about open water. It was a great relief when they sighted the warship, H.M.A.S. *Sydney*, exactly where they had asked for her in case of need. That sea, they knew, had sharks in it. They were doing eighty-three miles an hour. Splendid! Then Darwin—and world fame. The duration of the journey was just under twenty-eight days, with an actual flying time of 135 hours.

There had been a frantic scramble in Australia to clear some landing grounds for the winners to land on. One of the Middle East pilots had been taken on by the Commonwealth Government to survey and establish aerodromes on the route south from Darwin to Melbourne. Wilmot Hudson Fysh found that travelling along the ground from one prospective landing ground to another was far more difficult than flying. With him was another ex-Air Force pilot, Ginty McGinness. They had a hair-raising trip through Queensland to Darwin, their overloaded Ford wallowing in watercourses, charging into trees, and needing to have tracks cut for it.

When at last they reached Darwin an aerodrome was cut under Hudson Fysh's direction. The residents were furious that a favourite big tree had been destroyed. Why didn't Fysh put his confounded landing ground somewhere else? Down at Newcastle Waters nobody wanted to work in the hot sun, so McGinness used his charm on the Aboriginal women who, for presents of red cloth and tobacco, laid out the landing strip for him.

In Parliament, a member demanded: Why had the aerodrome at Darwin cost £700 when that at Newcastle Waters had cost practically nothing? Why the big difference? By the time Hudson Fysh was officially checking in the Smiths' Vickers-Vimy at Darwin, McGinness had reached Cloncurry in Queensland. While laying out the airfield there he was also wooing the local landholders to put money into civil aviation. The great company of Qantas, the Queensland and Northern Territory Air Service, which began with McGinness and Fysh, is now an international airline with Sir Hudson Fysh as chairman.

Ross Smith returned to England to plan a flight around the world. Keith Smith was to go with him. When the day for testing the plane arrived, Keith Smith's train was late. He was late at the aerodrome and Ross Smith went up without him. A few minutes later, the crash of that plane ended the lives of Ross Smith and his companion, Bennett, a great plane craftsman. For even the most famous men flew only with a rainbow glory. The clouds gathered, the luck changed, and it was gone.

They laid out the landing strip.

Chapter Four

TO SHARE IN EVERYTHING

Sing we the two lieutenants, Parer and McIntosh,
After the War wishing to hie them home to Australia,
Planned they would take a high way, a hazardous crazy
    air-way;
Death their foregone conclusion, a flight headlong to
    failure,
We said. For no silver posh
Plane was their pigeon, no dandy dancer quick-stepping
    through heaven,
But a craft of obsolete design, a condemned D.H.nine;
Sold for a song it was, patched up though to write an
    heroic
Line across the world as it reeled on its obstinate stoic
Course to that southern haven.

A Time to Dance by C. Day Lewis

LIEUTENANT RAYMOND PARER tried to comfort himself
that if he seemed to be out of luck, it was just that he had
never been one of those dashing, swaggering types who
impressed people. He had always understood engines.
Even as an apprentice he was planning a new type of aircraft. When, in 1916, someone convinced the "heads" at
Point Cook that it might be a good idea to take in men
who knew engines and train them as pilots, instead of
always drafting army officers, Raymond Parer had been
among those who qualified by ability as a mechanic.

He had tried for a fighter squadron, but was told he
was more valuable as a test pilot ferrying aeroplanes to
France. He had never had a crash, never a serious
accident. Twice he just missed out when he was recommended for the Air Force Cross.

Then came the 1919 Air Race to Australia, and it looked as though he would miss out completely. He had written to or interviewed every plane manufacturer in England. "They seemed to think that a man to whom they were to entrust their machine and reputation should be a polished man of the world, well versed in all the tricks of business," he wrote bitterly. What he needed was a mate, someone impressive, who would make people take notice, a kind of human mascot who could crash through the opposition, where Parer would just shrug and go away.

"One night in camp," he wrote, "I met McIntosh—saw just his back at table and caught a glimpse of his face, and at once felt: Here is the man I want. A man is always measuring up the strength, the battling qualities of other men. I had been mentally weighing up every man I met, and directly I met McIntosh, I felt: Here is one of the battlers, a man who goes after everything he wants and gets it."

McIntosh, a red Scot, was a ferocious, looming giant. He spread alarm. "He had a happy manner with obstinate beings," his friend noted, "of immediately seeing how unreasonable they were to oppose him; then they soon saw it too." One time in France the pair got petrol, "after Mac had threatened to kill the fat petrol-keeper". On another really desperate occasion, "Mac had to appear to lose his temper twice" before he overawed the opposition.

McIntosh, who had been a timber-getter in Western Australia, had struggled hard, after Gallipoli, to get into the Air Force. He invented an aerial bomb which was so good that he was asked what he wanted as a reward. "Just to get into the Air Force," he said. But by the time he qualified as a pilot, people, who did not realise that McIntosh was there, had declared an Armistice. He had only flown a plane once; he didn't know any navigation, he wasn't a mechanic, but he was willing to go with Parer.

"D'you mean as a mechanic?" He didn't like that idea.

"No, if we get away on this flight, we go as equals. I can be my own mechanic, if necessary, but we share in everything, each to do his own part, and if there is anything to be made out of the flight, we share that too."

In the air, Parer was to be in command. On the ground, McIntosh would handle all "business arrangements", such as dealing with persons in alien parts who had neglected to learn English, or discouraging Arabs with a Mills bomb while Parer tinkered with the engine.

Mac really changed Parer's luck for him. They were sitting in a stuffy hotel after interviewing a representative of yet one more aeroplane firm. "Forget about him," Mac dismissed the plane manufacturer. "He's just stringing you along. They're all waiting to see if Ross Smith falls into the sea. If he does you get a plane the day after. If he doesn't they've saved their money."

The door swung open and a friend of Mac's was there, asking why they were looking so fed up. As soon as he heard the tale he insisted they must see Peter Dawson. "He's not only a sportsman, one of the best; he's that strange thing, a generous millionaire." They could go back to Glasgow with Mac's friend and he'd introduce them to Peter Dawson.

Mac was tough, but he nearly had heart failure when the whisky magnate reached for his cheque book. "Buy the plane," Dawson commanded. Now they knew the oil company would supply them with petrol for the journey.

Later Peter Dawson asked if they had the plane they really wanted. They hesitated, then confessed they had set their hearts on a DH9, but didn't like to ask for the few extra hundred pounds. "Why didn't you say so? If you can risk your lives, I can risk £1,000." No, he didn't want them to scatter leaflets advertising whisky. He was just doing a little gambling.

They named the plane PD9 for Peter Dawson, their good friend. In a little bracket was screwed a bottle of his whisky which they presented to the Australian Prime Minister, William Morris Hughes, when they arrived in Melbourne. With all the mishaps and splintering smacks to land the bottle rode secure. When they were nearly sucked into the crater of the volcano of Vesuvius while McIntosh was trying to win a photography award, in the

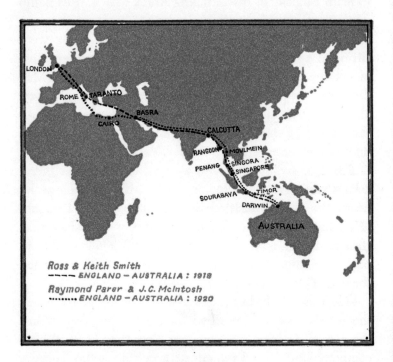

desert, soaring over the sea, faithfully untouched the bottle remained, unbroken.

Ross and Keith Smith reached Darwin, in the Northern Territory of Australia, while Parer was still testing PD9. Now the red tape really unwound. The race, the authorities declared, was over. Anyway, McIntosh was a Scotsman even if he had fought as an Australian. The plane was not fit for the trip. When two telegrams arrived, just before Parer and McIntosh set out, they left them unopened and took off in a howling gale, fearful only that they might be stopped. All the way to Egypt they dreaded that the military police were after them. Only there did they learn that permission had been given for the flight.

Landing in a field in France, Parer set off to find another wheel for the plane which had been badly damaged. He walked, he tramped, he found a wheel somehow, returning by a train which didn't leave until ten the next morning. He was met by a cart with a weary old horse which dragged him and the driver in lashing rain fourteen miles to where he found Mac cosily in front of a warm fire with the local schoolmistress, ready with warmth, food, and friendship. Mac and the blacksmith had strengthened the cracked undercarriage with handmade steel bars.

By the time they reached Italy they were out of money. They had started off with £18 of Mac's money and £25 belonging to Parer. They had not been able to afford flying kits at £40, but had managed to get some for £25. They did not like to impose on strangers but stayed at the cheaper hotels, walking miles to the aerodromes to save fares. Mac had a nightmare in which he vowed the macaroni was strangling him, but he had to get used to eating it.

They arrived in Naples on a rickety tram. Peter Dawson had told them to cable if they needed money. They didn't like to do this, but they waited for an answer, too broke to do anything else.

"Do you think we could have some wine?" the exhausted Parer asked, glancing wistfully at the gay crowd of diners.

"Well, we can't pay our bill," Mac chuckled. "We've

only thirty bob between us. So we might as well have
what's going."

They had the wine, and the British Consul advanced
them enough to live on. They did some sight-seeing,
marvelling at the bright throngs of people. "We felt so
shabby in our stained clothes." Then they were off again,
deafened by the roar of storms, the beat of the engine.
Death's wings beat with theirs, always a breath behind,
never quite overtaking. There was the time when the
plane caught fire and Parer dived it in such a way that
the flames blew harmlessly off the machine until he put
the blaze out.

Air was all ambushes round them, was avalanche, earthquake,
Quicksand, a funnel deep as doom, till climbing steep
They crawled like a fly up the face of perpendicular night
And levelled, finding a break
At fourteen thousand feet. Here earth is shorn from sight:
Deadweight a darkness hangs on their eyelids, and they bruise
Their eyes against a void: vindictive the cold airs close
Down like a trap of steel and numb them from head to heel;
Yet they kept an even keel
For their spirit reached forward and took the controls while
    their fingers froze.

They had not heard the last of death. When the mountains
    were passed,
He raised another crest, the long crescendo of pain
Kindled to climax, the plane
    took fire. Alone in the sky with the breath of their enemy
Hot in their face they fought from three thousand feet they
    tilted
Over, slide-slipped away—a trick for an ace, a race
And running duel with death: flame streamed out behind,
A crimson scarf of, as life-blood out of a wound, but the wind
Of their downfall staunched it; death wilted,
Lagged and died out in smoke—he could not stay their pace.

And there just below them was an aerodrome. "I
couldn't believe my eyes." They had lost their maps which

blew out of the plane when someone stole food from their locker and left it unlocked.

As they came down in Cairo, Mac roared exultantly, "Look at the crowds! About time too!"

But the crowds were there only to see Lord Milner's plane. Lord Milner welcomed them, and talked to them; but they were a little awkward with all these fine people. They got away as soon as they could.

They were always tired. After one terrible stretch, Parer confessed, "I felt a bit done up and so lay down and took pleasure in looking at the old bus. She had been chucking out the oil all over herself, and with her nose in the air and covered in streaks of oil she looked for all the world like an old war charger that had just been through a severe scrap."

How they loved and cherished that plane! To them it was a living being, a friend. It had a personality. They were sensitive about contemptuous glances at PD9. "Run over 'em," Mac yelled when a group of foreign officials ignored the plane. Parer sent his warhorse roaring at the group which scattered and showed a change of attitude—a nervous deference.

The great race to Cape Town was on, and Parer noted bitterly that Colonel Van Reyneveld used three machines. When one crashed, the Government simply flew him out another. The Italians were flying to Japan. "In every country from Rome to Japan the Italians had established bases with spare parts, new machines, mechanics." All at enormous cost, in great contrast to the take-it-or-leave-it race to Australia. The Italian airmen, when they smashed up a plane, simply climbed into a new one.

Parer carefully made a list of PD9's records. It was the first single-engine machine to cross the Mediterranean; the first single-engine plane to fly to Egypt; the only plane to cross from Palestine to Baghdad across the Syrian desert. All the others had taken the longer, safer route through Damascus and Palestine. Then it was the first single-engine plane to fly from England to Calcutta.

They became a little testy about reports that they had crashed when they had only come down to remedy some trifling thing that nearly killed them. "I was glad we had located and remedied a serious fault," Parer reported simply, on the occasion when the plane caught fire. It was just a badly jammed needle in the valve of the carburettor.

By the time they reached Penang, he admitted, "Having had no sleep I was very tired and flying was an effort." Their descent upset some polo players who cursed them

An interrupted polo game.

for interrupting the game, just as at Singapore they were dressed down for interrupting the golf, although they had permission to land on the racecourse. They were hustled off.

They were delayed at Singapore, waiting two days for a propeller and a radiator. When the radiator came, it was so unsuitable they had to make do with two car radiators. At Penang, they had managed to dismantle the seized engine, hoist it on to the bough of a tree, and with the help of one Chinese mechanic, rebuild it. They were "travelling without mechanics", the Official War Historian commented disapprovingly.

The awful landing grounds were responsible for the damage to the "dear old bus". At Moulmein, in Burma, the crowds had rushed them, and to avoid loss of life

They hoisted it on to the bough of a tree.

Parer took "evasive action" and had what he maintained was the only crash of the whole trip. They were *not* reckless and "intrepid birdmen"; they were two careful men, avoiding trouble and using every desperate expedient to do so.

They were greatly heartened by a cable from an Australian business man in the Dutch East Indies offering help. He had just bought a plane himself and proved a real friend. By now they had been informed that all the petrol supplies and stores laid down from Darwin to Melbourne had been used or sold. It was a little depressing, but they had two more records to make. Theirs was the longest non-stop Australian flight, from Timor to Darwin. And with good reason. When they landed at Darwin, the engine stopped dead. There was not a cupful of petrol left in the tank. Theirs was the only single-engine plane to fly from England to Australia.

"People of other lands gladly provided a guard for the machine," Parer noted. "We had to pay for a guard at Darwin." They were awarded the Air Force Cross for which Parer had already been twice recommended.

Southward still to Melbourne, the bourne of their flight they
    pressed,
Till at last near Culcairn, like a last fretted leaf
Falling from brave Autumn into the earth's breast,
D.H.9, their friend that had seen them to the end,
Gave up her airy life.
The Southern Cross was splendid above the spot where she
    fell,
The end of her rainbow curve over our weeping day:
And the flyers glad to be home, unharmed by that dizzy fall,
Dazed as the dead awoken from death, stepped out of the
    broken
Body and went away.

Yes, Parer admitted, it had been a bit of a strain. He bought a new plane, entered the aerial Derby and won it. He was later to be a pioneer aviator in New Guinea. People bothered him into writing a book, rather a dull little book about the trip from England. It was dedicated to "the late J. C. McIntosh" who had been killed flying in Western Australia.

Captain Matthews, for whom Parer and McIntosh had waited at Calcutta, cunningly thought out a variation on the early laps of the journey. He would cross Europe over the Balkans. The weather was, of course, abominable, and he was delayed a month at Mainz, then another week in Vienna. After that the bad luck changed to worse. Coming down in an open field they were surrounded by suspicious Yugoslavs, heavily armed. After four days as prisoners he and Sergeant Kay managed to snatch their papers and speed off in the plane one bullet shot ahead of their captors.

At Belgrade, they were given a soldiers' welcome by a mixed force of French and Serbs ready to toast them under the table, but when they enquired for petrol it appeared that nobody had any. Three weeks passed before a French pilot landed and was persuaded and argued out of enough fuel to get them to Bucharest where they landed in two feet of snow.

Matthews and Kay argued that things could not possibly get any worse, but a temperature of 46° below freezing point over Turkey disproved this. With varying mishaps

They dragged out their wrecked machine.

they nearly made Karachi, but were forced down by a tremendous sandstorm on a sea beach of the Persian Gulf. They dragged their wrecked machine out of the waves and Matthews, without food or water, set off along the burning sand to Bandar Abbas, while Kay stayed with the plane.

The British Consul got together a relief party and he with Kay decided to return by boat. But the storm drove the boat off into the islands of the Persian Gulf and they were marooned for three days. The two airmen repaired the longeron with some iron from a fence; an old iron bar served to splice the broken axle.

They crashed their way to Sourabaya, and then on to the island of Bali, but there with two smashed wings and a propeller warped by the rain and sun, they were forced to give up. They had worked so hard, patching and mending and contriving; Sergeant Kay with dengue fever; the engine's ball race smashed to pieces and replaced by one from a car. They had accomplished more than any two men in the way of resourcefulness and ingenuity, but that twisted propeller and the smashed wings, and no hope of replacements, had licked them.

The story of their flight and that of Parer and McIntosh made the more settled type of person feel that war birds might be intrepid, but were they quite right in the head? Ordinary people did not even want to do that sort of thing.

Chapter Five

THE BUBBLE REPUTATION

HE WAS ALWAYS being whirled up high by huge people, carried along, snatched into the air. He laughed with joy and they set him down; he stumbled after them, doggedly toiling, panting. "Hurry up if you want to come." Or they wouldn't let him go because he was too young.

He yelled at them, and they smacked him or caressed him, the huge mysterious crowd. Very early he learnt he had to attract their attention. "Look at Chilla! Isn't he wonderful! Do it again, darling!" The huge mysterious crowd were his mother and father, his two sisters, his four brothers, eight of them, all confident, gay, musical, fond of parties, singing, shouting. He was the little child in a grown-up family too old to play with him. He had to exhaust himself, make tremendous efforts because it was fun when they clustered around and petted him.

At school, with the golden curls his sisters loved shorn at last, he was a choir boy, looking angelic but often in trouble. He would rush his bicycle down the steepest hills never crashing, sure of his nerve. He liked fighting and he started fights; he fought like a threshing machine.

He was handsome and he knew it. Girls liked him; everyone liked him and wanted to be friends with him. But now he was an apprentice engineer with a motor bike, always too hard up to spend money on it. When he was eighteen, the war came and he fought with his mother to go. On his eighteenth birthday he was at the recruiting office, Charles Kingsford Smith, eyes blue, height five feet seven and a half inches. "I was acting sergeant for a few days but owing to my being only eighteen I was considered too young."

But now he was a despatch rider and could go tearing through traffic on a really powerful motor bike, people making way for him. And he had a cherished possession. He tossed away or lost other things he owned, but the photograph of Nellie Stewart, the beloved actress, the idol of the crowds, went with him to the Egyptian desert, to Gallipoli where he was in agonies of rheumatism. It was there in his plane over France when he lost two toes from a bullet wound and was lucky not to lose his life. He had his Military Cross and was an instructor when the war ended.

Now instead of being tossed into the air, he might be set down, grounded. But luckily there was the air race to Australia, and he had a fine plane, a good crew, every chance of winning. The newspapers said so. "The Rolls Royce Company," they reported, "saw Kingsford Smith, liked him, trusted him."

The plane had a new engine; he had congratulatory telegrams and good wishes. And then the order came that he was not to go. He and his crew were furious and fought the order to the highest quarters. "We feel we are responsible for the safety of these young fellows," the Prime Minister told the press. "*Young!*" Here it was again. "They would be sent to the best navigational school"; they didn't know enough navigation. Too young; left behind.

He went to America to get backing for a flight across the Pacific and all he could get was a dangerous, crowd-pleasing job as a stunt flyer. He grew tired of the people who, not satisfied with watching him "wing-walking" or hanging by his legs from undercarriages, waited to see his body carried off the field. He took on the role of "Flying Scarecrow", shooting ducks on the rice fields of California. He was always hard up, and too proud to let people know. But they had to know at home when he came back. "Going back with empty pockets, going back hard-up. Oh, it's then you know the meaning of humiliation's cup."

There were few jobs for pilots in Australia; about nine in the whole continent, someone reckoned, and they fell vacant only when a flyer hit a cloud with rocks in it. But over in Western Australia the first airline was starting, 1,211 miles from Geraldton across the lonely north-west hump of coastline to Derby in the Kimberleys, at the mouth of the Fitzroy River. When he passed his tests and went through a "refresher" course, his father gave him the fare to Perth.

The plane in which he was flying with Major Norman Brearley, founder of the airline, was forced down on a beach south of Broome and they fought a grim fight with a tide that has a rise and fall of twenty-eight feet. The tide was the stronger, and they returned to Perth with a dismantled plane on the little coastal vessel whose monthly visit was the only link between the north-west and the capital.

Another plane crashed with loss of pilot and mechanic, then another. The newspapers raised an outcry and the service was suspended. But Major Brearley was made of tough material, and West Australian Airways resumed. Often the temperature in the air was over the hundred mark. All kinds of crazy daring and teamwork were involved in keeping the machines going. Kingsford Smith's apprenticeship as an engineer, his long experience of engines, were now needed for bush repairs to planes. Anything might happen from carrying a sick Aborigine to laying out makeshift landing grounds or dodging a camel.

On his twenty-sixth birthday, in 1922, he flew from Geraldton to Perth, 270 miles in two and three-quarter hours, for what was then a cross-country speed record. The company's flying staff was small, and a return trip from Perth to Derby, stopping at the little pearl and beef ports, meant four days' steady flying at a stretch. Always Kingsford Smith was set in his determination to fly the Pacific.

Dodging a camel.

His fellow pilot, Keith Anderson, was just as keen as "Smithy" on the idea. His own ambition was to fly the Indian Ocean to Africa, but he was willing to fly the Pacific first. Another of "Smithy's" friends was Colonel H. C. Brinsmead, Controller of Civil Aviation, whose difficult task during these years was to convince flying men that a licence was not some stain on their character.

Colonel Brinsmead was inclined to look askance at one of the flying practices Smithy introduced to West Australia Airways. In a plane that could carry only two paying passengers, the relief pilot was odd man out. If he remained in the plane there was room for only one passenger. Smithy solved the problem by sitting, for hundreds of miles, on the lower wing with his arms around one of the struts. West Australian Airways took care to insure each of its pilots for £500 against death on duty.

After two years' flying on what was then the longest regular air route in the world, Smithy and Keith Anderson left to form a motor carrying company. It was gruelling hard work driving many hundreds of miles over tracks through spinifex with an overloaded trailer. Speed and

The joyrider.

skill and strength were needed. When they sold the business they had £2,300 clear profit. They could buy two Bristols from their old company and start an airline in New Guinea.

They tried to break the Perth-Sydney record on their flight to the east, but had to fly against winds which slowed them. The New Guinea venture was too hard a nut to crack. The landing grounds were just not there, and they had to make do with jobs as Inter-State Flying Services.

It was at that time Kingsford Smith met a lean, dark man called Charles Ulm. He was an organiser, dreaming great dreams of aviation and the company he could form to set his plans in motion. He was the ideal third partner for Anderson and Kingsford Smith.

But at first luck was against them. They tried without success for the rights to an airline from Adelaide to Perth. Then they decided that if they could break the round-Australia record—there had been only two previous flights —it would bring them a chance, perhaps, for their project of flying the Pacific. In their Bristol tourer, seven years old, they flew the 7,500 miles, breaking the previous record by thirteen days.

Better than that, the Premier of New South Wales, J. T. Lang, never very impressed by the Commonwealth Government's support of pioneer aviators, guaranteed £9,000 from New South Wales towards the expenses of the Pacific flight. The big, burly politician had been at Mascot aerodrome, Sydney, when Nellie Stewart placed laurel wreaths around the necks of Kingsford Smith and Ulm. They told him why they had flown round Australia and his response was prompt and generous.

Kingsford Smith, Ulm and Anderson set off for America; and for Smithy this was the springboard of his hopes. From now on no one would leave him behind.

The family had widened out to the Australian people. It was to be their approval that he sought, their demands he met. He was from now on the idol, the wonder child, who had to fly with more daring, higher, farther, soaring out of their sight, returning to their cheers.

Chapter Six

A MAN'S PLANE IS LIKE HIS HORSE

ABOVE THE TINY DOTS of men and dogs on the blazing white ice the sky stretched limitless and clear. Huge and clumsy in his furs, Vilhjálmur Stefánsson, the famous Arctic explorer, strode ahead paying little attention to the cheerful talk of his companion.

"Where I come from nobody *walks*," Hubert Wilkins jeered. "There's too much of Australia to footslog. What we ought to be doing is riding up in that sky in a plane."

Stefánsson plodded on.

"I'll do it, too, someday. They say you can't use planes in polar conditions. I'll show them." Wilkins bent down to wrench the sled runner over a hummock. "I never did like walking."

"First," Stefánsson said good-humouredly, "I'll teach you how to live on the ice so that when you fall out of your aeroplane you will not perish. It would be a pity," he chuckled, "for a young man like you not to walk back."

For three years Stefánnson tried to teach Wilkins the hard ways of the polar explorer. "He went on perfecting ways of walking," Wilkins said later. "In those three years I walked not less than 5,000 miles over the Arctic ice—probably much more."

It was in 1913 that Hubert Wilkins was first fired with the idea of flying over the Arctic and Antarctic ice. He left Stefánnson in the Arctic to join the Australian airmen in France. He had been flying since 1910 and was soon in charge of the photographic section of the Australian

Flying Corps, being awarded the Military Cross and Bar. After the war he joined Sir Ernest Shackleton on the *Quest* in that explorer's last expedition to the Antarctic.

Navigator, naturalist, astronomer, film photographer, airman and submarine commander, there was little Sir Hubert Wilkins would not attempt. But it was not until 1926 that he had his chance to use aircraft in the Arctic regions.

He wanted a dirigible balloon but, although he had the money available, none of the manufacturers would trust him with one of their precious machines. Wilkins's friend, the world-famous designer, Anthony Fokker, had a tri-motored monoplane, the very first of its kind. This he offered the explorer for the flight he intended—and finally made—from Point Barrow in Alaska to Spitsbergen, 2,000 miles across the polar sea.

No landing gear would have stood the crash.

"I bought the first 72-foot-winged, tri-engine Fokker monoplane ever made," Wilkins wrote. It had for those days enormous petrol storage; but this meant it had to take a great deal of punishment. "We considered the Fokker's landing gear weak for the maximum load we hoped to carry. It was sufficiently strong for all ordinary purposes, but no landing gear ever made would have stood the crash of our three-ton machine as it fell to the ground."

This was the first time Wilkins had taken the machine up in Arctic conditions. And there it was smashed. They kept strengthening and improving it. Wilkins's co-pilot regarded the Fokker with respect because of its weight, rather than liking. It was a case of setting a great race-horse to pull a milk cart. Wilkins decided that what he needed for his next attempt was a small plane so that he could be his own mechanic. The most generous-hearted of all modern explorers, he watched, without envy, the flight of Roald Amundsen and Nobile across the pole.

"I don't care who does it," he declared, "as long as people recognise that it is practical to cross the world by air over the Arctic."

But his first attempts had irritated him because he was cluttered up with newsmen and photographers and a great tail of followers, who all had to be supported and flown into Alaska and out. He had fallen in love with a Lockheed Vega, and wanted to sell the big Fokker so that he could buy this new beautiful plane. It would be just big enough to take him and Lieutenant Carl Eileson over the Arctic sea to Spitsbergen, and he could be his own business manager, workman, labourer, mechanic and navigator.

"Three Australians wished to fly from San Francisco to Hawaii," he wrote, "and then on to Fiji and Australia. Our big machine was well beyond their means but they wanted to buy it."

Although Wilkins was pressed for money he agreed to let them have it with only half the price down. The full price was £3,000.

"I have found that pilots, broadly speaking, fall into two classes," Wilkins once wrote. "A pilot will be either a slapdash, brilliant daredevil whom Lady Luck has seen

fit to favour in a miraculous way, or a steady, discerning,
cool-minded man, who flies steadily, meeting every condition with ready though deliberate action."

In 1927 Charles Kingsford Smith was the rarest of all
pilots, a man who had the best qualities of the daredevil
and the cool-minded man. He had enormous endurance,
concentration, patience, skill. He also had dash, charm,
and the ability to make other men like and trust him. The
ten years since the war had toughened and hardened him.

But during those long months of arrangements and dis-
appointments in San Francisco it often looked as though
the chance would again escape him. He, Charles Ulm and
Keith Anderson were just beggars on a grand scale; but
then Columbus and Drake had been that too.

Flights over the Pacific were being looked upon with
disfavour in the U.S.A. Seven men had been killed in the
race to Hawaii, and here were these three mad Australians proposing to fly over far greater stretches of ocean,
and in a land plane which they could not afford to buy.
The "big Fokker" had no engine in it. Wilkins explained
that it had been thriftily patched with a wing from his
other Fokker which had also crashed.

"In the reconstruction Wilkins had accidentally improvised a new type of plane," Kingsford Smith observed.

A Melbourne business man gave the three Australians
money to buy the Fokker, trying at the same time to persuade them not to make the flight. By paying only half
the price, they had enough to order the three engines. But
the factory which turned out the Whirlwind Wright
engines was so far behind with orders that it seemed as
though they would have to wait months.

Desperately they began to "pull strings". A U.S. naval
officer came to their help and won for them a promise of
early delivery. There was still all the fitting for the plane

to be purchased, the instruments, the radio equipment. They were running deeper and deeper into debt.

To earn some money, Kingsford Smith decided to make an attempt on the non-refuelling endurance record, which then stood at 52 hours 22 minutes. The *Southern Cross*, as the big Fokker was now called, had to be equipped with new axles for she was to lift the heaviest load of petrol ever carried by a plane of her size.

Her tanks would carry 1,522 gallons, but this meant she weighed seven tons instead of the five they had calculated; and she was then one of the largest planes in existence. Even the brakes were stripped off to reduce weight. The tail had to be strengthened and special flexible petrol pipes to resist vibration were fitted. The wheels and tyres were outstandingly strong.

They were halfway down the 4,900-foot runway before even the tail of the *Southern Cross* began to leave the ground. Three-quarters of the way, and roaring at ninety miles per hour, it seemed that the overloaded plane must crash into a bank, or levee, at the end of the runway. Without brakes, there was no choice but to charge it full throttle. A hundred yards away, Kingsford Smith and his co-pilot, Pond, pushed forward the controls and deliberately bumped the machine on the ground and over the levee.

In bitter cold they circled the air over San Francisco for two days and two nights, a fifty-mile circuit over San Francisco Bay. They couldn't smoke; they couldn't sleep. The intense cold meant that they were using more petrol than they had calculated on. On the morning of the third day they had to come down with the bitter knowledge that, not only had they failed to break the record, but they had failed to win the money they so desperately needed.

From lack of funds, Keith Anderson, thoroughly dis-

E

heartened, was forced to go home. The New South Wales Government would send no more money, and ordered Kingsford Smith to sell the *Southern Cross*. Kingsford Smith and Ulm could not even pay their hotel bill. They had no money to buy a meal or cigarettes. They decided that if they went to Los Angeles they might sell the plane to an oil company, but they did not have their train fare, so they flew the plane there instead; and failed to sell it. They had been six months working like fiends—for nothing. They were failures. Nobody would now even listen to them.

In this dark hour hope gleamed again. They were introduced to Captain G. Allan Hancock, an expert on navigation who was, luckily, a wealthy man. He not only took

He bumped the plane over the levee.

an interest in the Pacific flight and advanced them funds; he told them he would buy the plane and they could fly it.

Even with this windfall of enough money the risks were still enormous. If they came down in the sea, they might just possibly use the wing of the plane as a raft, but they knew what a slender chance that was. The longest stretch of overseas flight would be 3,128 miles, as far as from Sydney to Perth.

A great deal would depend on the navigator finding a

tiny, needle-point of island in a huge. blue haystack of sea. Captain Harry Lyon, their navigator, was an expert, and their radio man, Jim Warner, was another.

Now, even the highest powers of the U.S. Army and Navy were ready to assist Kingsford Smith and Ulm. But when it came to the last, they were dependent on the "big Fokker", the *Southern Cross*, for their lives; four men, squeezed and cramped between the petrol tanks, deafened by the engines, cold, sick from want of sleep.

In fair weather, with Kingsford Smith and Ulm in the cockpit, Lyon and Warner busy in the cabin, they set out for their first landfall of Honolulu. Upon Lyon fell the task of continually checking the course, the speed and the drift of the *Southern Cross*. Day drew into night and a new day came as they peered anxiously at the blue monotony of the sea.

Their landing at Honolulu was a triumph but they knew it was only the first of three stages. Ahead was the longest ocean flight ever to be attempted, farther than from London to New York. The *Southern Cross*, when fully refuelled, needed a long runway to take off, so within a couple of hours of landing on Wheeler Field, Honolulu, Kingsford Smith took the plane ninety miles to the beach on Kauai Island. The petrol had been taken there by sea but there were all the difficulties of refuelling in such conditions.

A few hours' sleep and at three o'clock in the morning they were up preparing for the dash along the sands. When they rose from the long beach a new set of anxieties revolved around finding the tiny dot on the map that lay over three thousand miles away. The storms came out to meet them, and Kingsford Smith knew that to fly around, to try to get over the storms, used up the *Southern Cross's* precious fuel. Torrents of rain beat down on them as they climbed, twisted, changed course in a frantic search for better weather.

"I had had a long, tiring night," Kingsford Smith wrote, "and handed over the controls to Ulm while I fell into an unsatisfying doze. I felt I could sleep for hours, but was soon jolted awake again by a sudden change of course. It brought me to my feet. I began to swear at Ulm for falling asleep at the controls, but he was grinning and pointing with his hand."

They were flying over Suva. In thirty-four and a half hours they had flown 3,138 miles. When they landed on the sports oval, dazed, just able to stumble out, they were stone deaf, and staggered off through the cheering crowd, while the police tried to clear them a path. Thousands of natives who had never seen a plane before came in from the outlying islands, and the flyers moved in a roar and bustle of welcome.

At midnight, unable to sleep, fearing the *Southern Cross* might not be safe, they went in borrowed kimonos to look at it, only to be warned off the sports oval by Fijian policemen with rifles at the ready.

Twenty miles away was Naselai Beach, "the best runway I had ever seen", wrote Kingsford Smith. But all the petrol for the last lap had to be brought there by boat. Would she do it; could the *Southern Cross* do it, the lap from Fiji to Brisbane, the capital of Queensland? By now the crew felt it was the plane that was making the trip, not the men. She was a magic wing of power.

Great gusts slashed at her as she jolted and bumped through the storms from Suva, staggering blind but roaring on. Ice-cold and sodden and stiff they endured. The logkeeper was too frozen to hold a pencil. Kingsford Smith took the *Southern Cross* to 7,000 feet but there was no relief from the storms. The glass windshields began to give way before the driving rain and ice. They were flying "stone blind".

Dawn brought some relief and they flew due west. The

Storms off Suva.

sun came out and warmed their frozen hands. When they swept in over the Australian coast they were 110 miles south of Brisbane. Suppose that had happened at Suva? Well, they just wouldn't be here.

The huge crowd at Eagle Farm aerodrome, Brisbane, waited to cheer them. "Get back," a policeman shouted. "This is no ordinary plane."

The *Southern Cross* had begun her career as a winged myth. She was from now on for Australians the unbeatable thoroughbred of the skies, to be cherished like some four-legged Melbourne Cup winner, a symbol of courage and speed.

At Sydney 300,000 people turned out to see the faultless and beautiful aeroplane and the men who had ridden the storms over 7,389 miles of ocean.

Chapter Seven

A STORM IS FULL OF BUMPS

THE TASMAN SEA is a storm breeder. Kingsford Smith's crew had, on the Pacific flight, flown over greater distances than the 1,630 miles that separated the Australian coast from New Zealand. But in 1928 there were no aeroplanes capable of flying at the heights which, today, give the passenger airliners a pleasant, monotonous passage over the Tasman.

To conquer the Tasman—and "Smithy" and Ulm planned in their first flush of victory to do just that—was like plunging into a blackberry bush. You did not expect to emerge without some scratches.

Five months before the *Southern Cross* surged in from her Pacific crossing, Lieutenant John Moncrieff and Captain George Hood had aroused keen interest in the public, and fears among the Civil Aviation authorities, when they were reluctantly allowed to set out on the first attempt to fly to New Zealand. The Prime Minister of New Zealand and the Prime Minister of Australia, neither of them timorous men for each had won the Military Cross, were divided on the wisdom of the flight. The flyers had argued that "the pioneer effort must be made sometime". The New Zealand newspapers and people excitedly agreed.

The two New Zealand airmen, unable to raise the money to buy a flying boat, brought a small Ryan monoplane to Australia by ship, assembled it, hurried to Richmond aerodrome forty miles from Sydney, and with some ten hours' test-flying, were ready to set off. The wild gales of the Tasman were somehow waved aside with the Government's lifted ban on the flight, and preparations went forward in New Zealand for the welcome. The flyers started with some cakes of chocolate, and a defective radio, and were never seen again.

When Kingsford Smith announced his intention to fly to New Zealand, he said, "We are not undertaking this flight to show that we can do what New Zealanders failed to do. We are undertaking it to show that the attempt made by Hood and Moncrieff was not impracticable."

Smith had decided that the enormous prestige he had won should be the foundation of a passenger service. He and Charles Ulm were working, not for speeches at banquets, but for the setting up of permanent airlines which would link all the cities of the continent—yes, and New Zealand—with Europe and America. The two of them would build Australian National Airways. New Zealand would be the last stopping place of the England-Australasia route.

"Nothing is to be rushed," Ulm said. The radio, one of the weak points of the Moncrieff-Hood tragedy, was given special attention. As a gesture to the people of New Zealand, the wireless operator was a New Zealander, T. H. McWilliams. A new propeller was fitted and exacting tests were made, including a record non-stop flight from Melbourne to Perth, 2,090 miles. As they flew back above the high cliffs of the Great Australian Bight, H. A. Litchfield, the navigator, set a course for Adelaide by the stars, and McWilliams made contact with Adelaide radio, 1,350 miles away.

In Sydney, the *Southern Cross* waited and waited for fine weather. When the forecast was "Practically clear over the Tasman" they set off, everything in perfect order.

A little over 500 miles out to sea the storm met them. Kingsford Smith tried to outclimb the clouds woven with lightning. "He pushed the *Cross* to 10,000 feet. She would not climb another inch." But the storm extended thousands of feet above the plane. Rain squalls were tearing at them from every direction. Sheets of water swept along the wings. By running the motors at full throttle Kingsford Smith kept the engines hot and lessened the chance of the rain putting the ignition system out of order.

"It was much worse than the Suva-Brisbane flight," he wrote later. "In the thin air at 10,000 feet a heavily laden machine is hard to handle in the best of weather." They had to fight to keep the plane on course.

But worse was to come—ice. The *Southern Cross* began to sink beneath the weight of ice coating the wings. This was before the New Zealander, Arthur Clouston, as a test pilot risked his life in experiments to see what ice did to a plane, and equipment was installed to meet the danger. In these years ice, adding half a ton to the weight of the plane, clogging the wing surfaces and over-heating the engine, was often a sentence of death.

In the *Southern Cross* they were flying blind. Suddenly the airspeed indicator went down to zero. While the pitot-head was blocked with ice, the *Cross* fell from 8,000 to 2,500 feet. Here the storm was wild, but the plane gradually shook off her frozen load. In the gusts above the sea the men were tossed about "like boots in a sack".

"The whole machine was charged with static electricity," wrote John Stannage, one of "Smithy's" friends. "A flash and the three propellers were enshrouded in an eerie glow, blue, malevolent and full of hidden menace; another flash and the glow was gone. A small spark and those five hundred gallons of petrol would send them sky-rocketing in a chaos of flying debris."

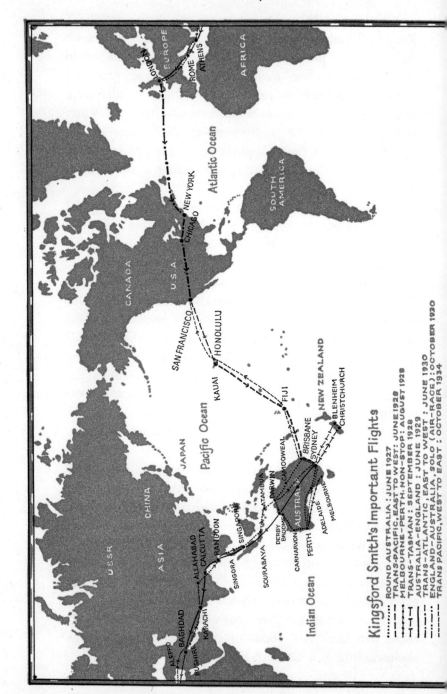

Kingsford Smith's Important Flights

...... ROUND AUSTRALIA : JUNE 1927
– – – TRANS-PACIFIC, EAST TO WEST : JUNE 1928
–•– MELBOURNE-PERTH, NON-STOP : AUGUST 1928
–┬– TRANS-TASMAN : SEPTEMBER 1928
– – AUSTRALIA-ENGLAND : JUNE 1929
–••– TRANS-ATLANTIC, EAST TO WEST : JUNE 1930
–•••– ENGLAND-AUSTRALIA, SOLO (AIR-RACE) : OCTOBER 1930
–••••– TRANS-PACIFIC, WEST TO EAST : OCTOBER 1934

Charles Ulm handed Kingsford Smith a note to say that lightning had burnt out the two radio sets; and, in the tossing plane, McWilliams was flung to and fro across the cabin, still trying, as radio men will, to repair the useless equipment.

Waiting thus for instant death is something that must be experienced to be understood. Terror is the breath in a man's mouth; even the bravest falter, expecting the end of the torture of time that goes on and on. The storm flung the four of them, Kingsford Smith, Ulm, McWilliams and Litchfield, as a cat throws up a mouse in its claws; while Kingsford Smith held the *Southern Cross*; steadied her in the still clinging ice.

With dawn they were still alive; the storm had eased and breaking the clouds were the great mountains of the land they looked for. The crossing of the Tasman had taken twelve hours, and the escort aircraft roared around them as they came to a perfect landing at Christchurch in the South Island.

McWilliams told the crowd simply, "The Tasman can be a rough place, and it was very rough." He added later, "Often it took both Smithy and Ulm to hold the controls. Without Smithy we wouldn't have got through."

A young man who kept a garage and a second-hand car business, drove a hundred and sixty miles, arriving just too late to see the landing of the *Southern Cross*.

"But there, still, was the *Southern Cross*," Air Commodore Clouston wrote later, "covered with oil and dust, squashed flies and midges, the exciting travel stains of the first flight across the Tasman Sea; and I knew as I walked slowly around the machine that I wanted to fly." One of Clouston's bravest record-breaking flights was to be from London to Cape Town and back again in five days; and in 1938 he was to break all existing flight records from London to New Zealand.

In Wellington, the capital of New Zealand, a tiny, pretty girl, who was a skilled pianist, decided that now the piano was only something to spread maps on. She must go to London and become a flyer. Less than ten years later, Jean Batten was to be the first woman to make the return flight, England-Australia; and to make the first direct flight from England to New Zealand.

With a difficult flight back to Australia behind him, Charles Kingsford Smith began to plan a new life. He regarded record-breaking only as a means to an end. He was not a "stunt" pilot, and all the luncheons and banquets meant very little to him.

Kingsford Smith was to other aviators as a great symphony conductor is to the players in the orchestra. He handled aircraft as a musician handles an instrument, with knowledge, love, skill and the extra sense of split-second timing that makes the expert in any profession.

He had the ability to move as the centre of a group, unique, and yet gathering around him the devotion, the casual loyalty, the friendship, of many men and weaving them into a working body. His early life as the darling of a large, noisy, talented family helped him to handle the problems of working with people. He could be persuasive, casual, get his own way, while fitting in with many complicated plans around him. He resolved he would get together a great fleet of planes, the men to fly them, the landing grounds, the engineers.

Chapter Eight

FAME IS A MAGNET FOR DISASTER

AFTER THE TREMENDOUS Pacific flight and the conquest of the Tasman Sea the reputation of Charles Kingsford Smith could not have been higher. Australian National Airways, the business planned by C. T. P. Ulm, would need new aeroplanes; and early in 1929 the details of a flight to England to purchase these planes were arranged.

The *Southern Cross* was overhauled; all the foreign permits and ground organisation were in order. With the same crew that he had on the New Zealand flight, Kingsford Smith set off contentedly from Richmond, New South Wales, for Wyndham, a new point of departure from Australia on the far north-west coast. The weather reports from Wyndham were good; the plane was roaring along smoothly, when tiny details began to mount up to a major catastrophe.

They found themselves forced down on a mudbank on an unknown coastal inlet, out of petrol, with no food except a consignment of baby food they had planned to deliver at Wyndham. And such tiny mishaps brought them there. First, the radio aerial was lost; but they did not turn back because they could still send messages, and if they returned, they might have trouble landing the plane with her heavy burden of petrol. Then, when they had crossed the Overland Telegraph, two-thirds of the way across the continent, the weather began to change.

Another weather report had been sent them, which

of course they could not hear, that torrential rain and dense cloud had suddenly appeared. By the time they reached the north-west they were flying blind. "It was a horrible night."

Dawn brought them to the coastline William Dampier had navigated two hundred and thirty years before, a jagged coast "with plenty of angry sea". They searched vainly for Wyndham. "I have never seen," wrote Kingsford Smith, "such an inhospitable terrain of ravines, roaring torrents, cliffs, heavy timber, and an entire absence of habitation." Their petrol was being used up little by little.

After several hours' flying along the coast they caught sight of a group of huts, a little mission station. Ulm dropped a weighted note:

"Please point direction of Wyndham."

The excited natives pointed in the wrong direction, to a patch of clear ground where they thought the *Southern Cross* might land; but, baffled, the flyers changed course.

Another mission station was more helpful. The missionaries laid out white sheets and towels to mark a course; but also the ominous figure, "250". Two hundred and fifty miles was beyond the reach of their remaining petrol!

Kingsford Smith again changed course and flew for a hundred miles. Then, with one tank left, unable to locate the mission again because of poor visibility, he brought the *Southern Cross* safely to ground, on a mudbank, at a minimum landing speed of fifty miles per hour!

All through their misadventures McWilliams had been sending a calm and coherent account of the changes of course. "The dear old bus had again saved us." Miraculously, they were alive, to be eaten by sandflies and mosquitoes, with the *Cross* sunk deep in the mud, but luckily above high tide level. Kingsford Smith had brought her to a halt a hundred yards before a large tree. They had been twenty-eight and a half hours in the air.

The emergency rations in the locker had been filched by some casual thief, and so all they had to eat were the tins of baby food which they rationed out a spoonful at a time. With this and the brackish water they made a sort of gruel.

They tried to light fires, but grew weaker as they laboured day after day with green wood that hardly burned. There was a flask of coffee and a small bottle of brandy in the *Cross*, so they christened the inlet "Coffee Royal". Over the radio came directions to light three *big* fires, each 500 yards apart, in the form of a triangle. Three big fires, with green wood, over a distance of nearly a mile, when, after four days, they were barely able to crawl!

All the time they were trying to get the wireless transmitter going. From the radio they learnt the movements of the *Canberra* plane searching for them. But, in the cities, few expected them to be found alive. The last message from McWilliams had been: "About to make a forced landing in bad country."

Keith Anderson, who had been so exasperated at missing the Pacific flight that he could hardly forgive his old friend's success, set out to look for him. For two years he had flown with "Smithy" in the north-west. Unfortunately, Anderson did not tell anyone, except his backer, of his proposed flight.

Anderson and his mechanic, H. S. Hitchcock, flew from Richmond to Alice Springs where they spent the night. Then they met the same tiny, creeping misfortunes that add up to danger. Their plane was overloaded with petrol, a minor fault put one of the four cylinders out of action, and the remaining three could not keep the plane in the air. Anderson brought his plane down safely in a small

They grew weaker day by day.

clearing in thick mulga scrub, but there, repairing the plane, keeping a record to the last, they died of thirst.

These two brave men had perished; tremendous efforts had been made before Kingsford Smith and his crew were found, alive, though living on gruel and snails. In the rescue plane commanded by Captain Leslie Holden was J. W. Stannage, Smithy's old friend and wireless operator.

"The country over which we were flying was indescribably dreadful," wrote Stannage, "and we were careful to carry an experienced bushman in case we were forced down and had to make our way back to civilisation. On the morning of the third day, we were flying at 3,000 feet when we suddenly sighted two small white patches on the edge of a swamp. Holden came lower, and then we made out the wing of a plane. We saw two figures come stumbling down the hill from a signal fire, and then two others emerged from under the plane.

"As I leaned out of the window, excitedly watching the scene below, I tapped out a message with the other hand: 'Found! Found! Found' "

They threw out some food and returned to Wyndham to take out next day mosquito nets, citronella, shoes. In the mud Kingsford Smith wrote: "CIGS". They dropped all the cigarettes there were in the plane. It was five more days—the monsoon rains were over—before the heat had dried the mud sufficiently for a light plane to land, and more before the *Southern Cross* had enough petrol to travel to Derby. They had been nineteen days at "Coffee Royal".

But, in the cities, the newspapers which had built up the Big Story, turned on Kingsford Smith in a peculiar way, though one well known to Wizard Stone and young Bert Hinkler in the years before the war. There was an outcry that the forced landing was a "fake", a publicity stunt. The man who, a little time before, had been the darling of the nation, was abused as a cheap sensation-monger. It was a hideous and undeserved situation, but no one could have been more affected by it than Kingsford Smith.

They had caught him up, raised him high; then dropped him down. It was his old childhood situation. Bewildered, sickened by Anderson's death, by the sneers that clung even when a Committee of Enquiry publicly cleared him, he had spent racking hours in the witness box. Why had he not poured the remaining eighteen gallons of oil in the *Southern Cross* on the smoke fires? Black smoke, he answered, does not show clearly against a dark background wall of jungle. Why had they left without emergency rations? They did not know they had been stolen from the plane. Was not going without a wireless aerial "an error of judgement"? Why did they not have more tools and spare parts for repairs?

No one asked why they should risk a machine worth £10,000 in a forced landing just for a newspaper story. And, as an afterthought, their lives. It was a miracle they had landed at all. But all this, the "Coffee Royal" Enquiry, left a bad taste, a bitterness in the lives of the four men. It was a harder experience than when they had circled round and round, fifteen feet from the ground, over Anderson's plane, unable to land, unable to do more than drop food to the body they saw lying beneath the wing.

But they recovered. The *Southern Cross* was put in trim again. Australian National Airways was a going concern; and next time they set out, the tools, much more water, a shot gun, emergency rations—nothing was overlooked. They left the day after the Committee made its report public.

This time they flew to Derby which Kingsford Smith knew well; and from Derby to Singapore, in tricky rain and cloud, a flight of 2,020 miles—the first time a plane had gone from Australia to Singapore without a stop. Then from Singapore they pressed on to Rangoon where they repaired the port engine which had been worrying them. At Calcutta, a large bamboo stake had been driven into the ground overnight. In the grey dawn, Kingsford Smith did not see it until twenty feet away when he made a desperate effort to lift the plane over it. He succeeded, but the stake tore a great hole in the underbody.

Allahabad was frying at 118° in the shade when they refuelled, but at Karachi they bathed in the river and planned to reach London in stages that would take them five days.

Their worst hindrance was in Athens where they were held up by the aerodrome officials forbidding their departure. Yes, they had permission to land; but where was their permission to leave? One of those maddening pieces of stupidity. They left, anyway, saying that they were merely going to taxi the plane and test the ground. They just roared away not bothering much what the men on the ground might do or not do about it. They weren't coming back that way, they had decided.

The *Southern Cross* was cutting down the distance, cutting down the time for the route. When they arrived in London, their record time was 12 days, 18 hours. The *Cross* had suffered a little from overloading and from the heat of the deserts and the tropics. It went to Holland for a loving overhaul at the Fokker works, free of charge.

In California, before Kingsford Smith had started on his Pacific flight, he had asked Anthony Fokker, "Do you think we can do it—in a Fokker plane?" The great designer had replied drily, "Of course you can do it in a Fokker plane—if you can fly." Anthony Fokker now subscribed £1,000 for the flight Kingsford Smith had planned across the Atlantic.

But while the details of the flight were being arranged, Kingsford Smith was off again across the Atlantic to America by ship, then to the Pacific coast and back to Australia. It was on the Pacific voyage that he met his future wife. He had been married once before in Western Australia but the marriage broke up. A pilot who flies shifts day after day, whose home is a hotel room, has little chance of building family happiness.

A hero, with the beginnings of his own airline, is in a more promising position. Even so his future wife could not regard the Atlantic flight without anxiety. There had been many attempts to fly the Atlantic east-west, some ending in tragedy. There had never been a plane to make a successful crossing to the United States. It was agreed that Charles Ulm should stay in Australia to tend the fortunes of National Airways. On the Atlantic flight, Kingsford Smith would take Evert van Dyke, a Fokker pilot, as a tribute to the Fokker Company.

In London he met Stannage who asked, "I heard something about an Atlantic flight? What about me?" He was immediately added to the crew.

The *Southern Cross*, now gleaming silver and blue, took off from Portmarnock Beach, in the Irish Free State. It was a beach with stretches of sand, hard and level for miles. They followed the course of the Great Circle, from Galway to Cape Race, on the tip of Newfoundland. It was the season of icebergs and they did not see a single ship after they left the coast of Ireland.

All went well until the afternoon. Then, with the wind against them, they flew into mist so thick they could not see the water two hundred feet below. The three compasses pointed in different directions. All through the night they battled on surrounded by fog with the unspoken fear that they might fly aimlessly until they ended in the sea. "It was the longest period we had ever been forced to fly completely blind." For twenty-four hours Kingsford Smith and Van Dyke had sat, cramped and cold. In the cabin Stannage constantly feared lest his aerial be dragged into the sea.

Not till they climbed again to 3,500 feet did the compasses return to normal. The fog belt moisture off Newfoundland was charged with electricity. The appeals for guidance from the Newfoundland aerodrome were unanswered, but a rift in the mist allowed the navigator to identify the coast.

On the flight south to New York Kingsford Smith saw 1,000 feet below a thirty-foot shark, the largest he had ever seen. It was an ominous symbol swimming along

in the calm, clear water. Then came the cheers from the
sailors of the U.S. Navy as they swept low over the decks
of ships at manoeuvres, and in New York the grandest
welcome they had ever had.

They rode through streets of deafening crowds and
clamorous pressmen and photographers. In Washington
they were received by President Hoover at the White
House, and their flight across America was a succession

Below was the thirty-foot shark.

of triumphs. When Kingsford Smith brought the *Southern
Cross* down at Oakland Airport, in California, she had
completely circled the globe, crossing and recrossing the
Equator. Never before had an aeroplane made such a
journey.

Before he returned to Australia his heart was set on breaking one more record, Bert Hinkler's wonderful solo flight
from England to Australia in fifteen and a half days. He
had arranged to return to Amsterdam before he set off
in the small Avro Avian sports biplane which he called
the *Southern Cross Junior*.

But in Amsterdam he had first an appendix operation
and then a bout of influenza. He was anxious to get back

to Australia for his wedding, and because C. W. Hill had set out ahead of him intent on breaking the record first. Kingsford Smith overtook his rival, relentlessly racing through mist, wind and rain. "The secret of success depends in the perfection of one's plans, the capacity for monotonous endurance, and first-hand knowledge of the territories over which one passes."

Once when he was a very young man—was it so few years ago?—Charles Kingsford Smith had been stopped by a Prime Minister from making this very flight. Nobody and nothing would stop him now. It was almost dull, apart from a broken bolt at Singapore; well, he knew the country—by now he knew the whole world stretched out and wheeling green and blue below him.

He thought as he crossed the Timor Sea of Ross and Keith Smith, the first who had gone over it by air. It was only eleven years since they had made the flight that he had felt even then was his own.

At Atamboea, on the island of Timor, there was a difficult landing ground; and there also was Hill whose plane had crashed just as he was about to take off on the last lap to Darwin. Hill had been a prisoner-of-war with Thomas White in Turkey; a brave man, able to take any disappointment with calmness, he immediately offered Kingsford Smith a light rubber boat in the event of trouble over the Timor Sea.

They spent the evening together, yarning, and next afternoon Kingsford Smith swept in over Darwin. He had done the journey, alone, in ten days and had beaten Hinkler's record of two years before. "The flight had shown," he observed, "that there is really nothing in these long air trips beyond the reach of the ordinary pilot."

He was trying to prove that the air links around the world were not just possible but inevitable. It was a matter of improving the organisation on the ground. What did it matter if he was tired, atrociously tired? Bert Hinkler cabled congratulations; so did the King of England. Now there was little left for him to conquer.

He would be an air pilot on a grand scale. As director of his company he would make the first regular flight in the New Year when the service began between Melbourne and Launceston in Tasmania, across Bass Strait. The *Southern Cross* was being shipped home from California. 1931 was to be a happy, happy year, married and with a settled home at last, Honorary Air Commodore of the Royal Australian Air Force.

He was up in the heights again, caught up once more, praised, borne on men's shoulders. Was it little more than a year since they were starving with the mosquitoes on that mudbank? The loneliness, the dirt, with death drawing their blood in the humming cloud of miseries?

How swiftly he came up! How suddenly, he knew now, he could drop!

There was a play of Shakespeare's in which King Henry VI said:

> They that stand high have many blasts to shake them.
> And if they fall, they dash themselves to pieces.

Chapter Nine

AN AIRLINE IS SUPPOSED
TO MAKE MONEY

DOWN BY BOTANY BAY, with its wide, wind-swept waters and swamps, was reclaimed pasture land that the cattle for the nearby abattoirs had grazed smooth and neat. One of its attractions to Nigel Love, who came back from World War I to start the Australian Aircraft and Engineering Company, was that the "bullock paddock" was cheap. That made the 160 acres ideal for Australia's first civil flying field. All you needed were some sheds.

It was, nevertheless, something of a surprise to H. E. Broadsmith who, as agent for Avro, had joined Captain Nigel Love and Lieutenant Warnford to make aeroplanes in Australia. English aerodromes did not have a smell from the boiling-down works blowing across them, nor were they approached by a road that was just potholes edging a set of tram tracks. However, the "river" and the bay would be useful for seaplanes.

The first large load of dismantled aeroplane, drawn by a team of horses, bogged inside the gate of the bullock paddock. The enormous packing case, and other cases which came after, formed a handy home for the caretaker, also stores and offices while the aeroplane remained under canvas. People came not only to see it. They liked to touch it. They poked holes in it with their fingers and umbrellas.

Officially, Mascot Aerodrome opened in 1920, in time for the flight of Ross and Keith Smith to Australia. Crowds, in those days and for long after, seemed not to notice that planes needed a clear space to land upon. As soon as an arrival was sighted they would swarm out on the landing ground.

On the great day of the arrival of Ross and Keith Smith in Sydney, so unruly was the welcome that Broadsmith, trying to struggle into the official tent, was thrust into the milling, struggling crowd; and by the time he had explained to the police, the official party had gone off to the city.

Broadsmith was never a pushful man, but intelligent and rather shy. One of his great enthusiasms was for Australian timber. He rode and walked over great stretches of wild country, testing and selecting the types he thought would be suitable for struts and frames. The

Plane inspectors.

British manufacturers, however, looked with a jealous eye on the poor little company which, in spite of an order for six planes from the Australian Government, was soon ruined. Its creditors received the money which, if it had been paid a little earlier, would have saved the partners. Selling a plane to the Government, with all the departmental delays, was a heart-breaking business.

Broadsmith, who had come with such high hopes, found himself the sole worker in the factory, even sweeping it out. His wonderful timber was sold for a song and probably, he thought bitterly, used for firewood. The materials and aeroplane parts were snapped up at a bargain price by the Air Force.

Even Broadsmith was snapped up by the Department of Civil Aviation; but he was not happy as their consulting engineer and returned to England. He was back in 1927, submitting designs for an Australian plane to the Larkin Aircraft Company, but the Government imported an expert from England, who declared that there was no need for planes to be built in Australia.

For the next twenty years, at least, contracts were given only to British manufacturers; and it was considered unpatriotic to hint, as Kingsford Smith did, that while Britain might build the best fighting planes, the Americans were far ahead with commercial planes.

Broadsmith came back at least five times to try to develop aeroplane building in Australia. In 1938, when he was offered a post as head of the Commonwealth Aircraft Corporation, the offer came too late. By that time he had made his name and position in England and could not accept.

Mascot continued to be the home of the commercial flyer. When Kingsford Smith's Australian National Airways went into operation, his planes took off from the old Mascot aerodrome which even now, as the great Kingsford Smith Airport, is still approached through a heavy odour of hides, tallow and soap. The runway at Mascot was never long enough for the *Southern Cross* to lift herself into the air with a full load for the record, long-distance flights, which were commenced from the Royal Australian Air Force grounds at Richmond.

The Air Force was the only body in Australia in the 1920's capable of training pilots and it supplied them to the three aviation companies. The twelve months' course, by a series of miracles, changed young men whose only aim in life seemed to be to frighten everyone into heart failure, from would-be suicides into responsible and skilful pilots.

The pilot had to be not only resourceful but a mechanic of no mean ability. Arthur Affleck, one of the men who flew with Qantas in the early days, tells how the lone pilot, at some little bush airstrip, would start the engine in the cold morning by soaking two pads of muttoncloth in petrol, and applying them to the engine breathers. He would twist the propeller for compression, rush around and duck under the wing, leap into the plane, crank the starting handle, which was usually in some inconvenient place, and then find he had to do it all over again.

One morning, he was so desperate after an hour that he took out all the spark plugs and warmed them in a little petrol fire on the blade of a shovel, filling the warm plugs with petrol squirted in with a syringe used for dosing cows. The engine started at once.

But another time when he was following his usual routine with the petrol-soaked pads, the engine backfired and the whole front of the plane cowling went up in flames. He had to smother the fire with a tarpaulin.

Even if a plane started, there were so many things that could go wrong. Admittedly, pilots were not often killed in crashes, but that might only have been that they were

made of very tough material, tougher than the planes
which were expensive, even if they were only wood,
canvas and wire.

An airstrip which a station owner might describe as
"dead level" would be found to have holes and stumps,
with cows wandering over it; cows had a passion for eating the fabric off plane wings.

A pilot would fly along, keeping his sight on the ground
for a railway line or the marks that might indicate a
road. In huge stretches of Australia these were just not
there. If he saw a house, he landed and asked for directions. The three companies, Qantas in Queensland, West
Australian Airways, and Larkins Australian Aerial Transport, agreed that Australia was the place where planes
came to die.

Horrie Miller, the head and front of West Australian

Warming the spark plugs.

Airways, a magnificent pilot and also a mechanic who could get any wreck off the ground, would set off with his tool-kit to the scene of the smash, and camp there until, single-handed, he had built the plane again to the stage where he could bring it in for repairs.

The Department of Civil Aviation had as its first inspector a Scotsman, Jock Baird, who worked under the famous Colonel Brinsmead, Controller of Civil Aviation until Brinsmead was killed in a crash in Siam.

Jock Baird found himself on one occasion going to inspect a crash near Port Hedland, W.A., and the only way he could get there was by camel. The temperature was up to 120°, and the camels had been daubed with engine oil to prevent ticks. Combined with the original smell of camel the engine oil brought out an odour so noticeable that even the heat took second place.

At another time Baird wrote a hot letter to an airline, telling it that he would not issue a certificate of airworthiness to that company's planes and the only thing to do with them was to burn them. Strangely enough a fire broke out soon after and the planes were in the fire.

Navigation was still in a primitive stage, and one passenger became so irritated with the pilot losing his way that they finished the journey with two ropes tied to the pilot's arms. When the man in the seat behind pulled on the left rope, the pilot turned left; when he pulled on the right rope, he turned right.

A government subsidy of a few pennies a mile was what an airline looked to for bread and butter. Little companies struggled along taking the stray passenger or joy flight; and even the governments, determined to keep planes from competing with the State-owned railways, admitted that aviation had its advantages for delivering mail or people to hospital.

The real pioneers were the oil companies, which, over

hair-raising roads, somehow managed to deliver oil and aviation fuel to little, lonely saltpans with a windsock flying over a galvanised iron shed. For long-distance flights, such as those made by Kingsford Smith and Gordon Taylor, fuel arrangements were vital; and they were never the weak link. The man with the petrol got there somehow.

It was not until 1929 that the east-west airmail began with fifty-one bags of mail proudly shipped in the *City of Perth*. Night-flying beacons were set up; and the Sydney-Perth Air Race of that year, with seventeen starters, marked one more point of advance.

The year before the three main companies had sixty-four commercial pilots registered and eighty-seven civil aircraft. The Civil Aviation Department was closing a tighter hand on the leftover daredevils and their unfortunate ruins of planes. But many years would pass before the actual landing grounds in the bush were any more than a pilot's nightmare.

On one occasion a pilot, George McCausland, was flying a Civil Aviation inspector out of Hall's Creek in Western Australia, when the engine coughed and went dead. George landed the plane in a paddock full of three-foot stumps that had been "cleared" to give "a better approach" to the aerodrome. They hit a stump with a shattering crash: another job for Horrie Miller and his tool-kit!

"That was a beaut, George," the passenger remarked, unstrapping himself. "Are you all right?"

He was talking to himself. The pilot was not in the plane; but how he got out was a mystery because there was no door where he was sitting, and certainly no body had flown past in the air. George was outside the plane with a dazed look, not knowing how he got there. Close examination showed a crack like a hairline in the body where it had opened smartly, catapulted the pilot out, and closed again so neatly that only the search revealed what had happened.

Australian National Airways, into which Kingsford Smith and Ulm put the money they had made from the flights over the Pacific and the Tasman, piled up three-quarter of a million miles of accident-free flying. There were the *Southern Moon, Southern Star, Southern Sun* and *Southern Sky* plying between the capital cities.

And there was the *Southern Cloud*, a name never forgotten in Australia in accounts of air disasters. Certainly the storm into which she flew over the great Kosciusko massif was the worst in thirty-one years; and that area was a wild jumble of river gorges and snow-covered mountains. With the radio warnings now available the *Southern Cloud* would have turned back; but, at that time, the Department of Civil Aviation, "for lack of funds", had none of the safeguards that flight has today.

It cost Australian National Airways £10,000 looking for the *Southern Cloud*; and after a fortnight the search was abandoned. Not until twenty-seven years later, in 1958, was the wreckage of the plane found in the Australian Alps.

Until then all that was known was that the company's senior pilot and eight passengers had died somewhere between Sydney and Melbourne; and although the enquiry found the company blameless, the loss of the *Southern Cloud* was a blow from which Australian National Airways, struggling in the grip of the depression, did not recover. People were just not flying. They did not have the money to fly; they did not care for what they now felt was the risk involved.

On top of the loss of the *Southern Cloud* came the news that the first airmail plane from England to Australia was grounded near Koepang, on the island of Timor. Kingsford Smith dashed off in the old *Southern Cross* from

Sydney to Darwin, across the Timor Sea. He brought the mail back to Darwin, loaded it on a Qantas plane, transferred the returned mail to England to the *Cross*, and was off again over the 517 miles of the Timor Sea, "The Ditch", as he now called it. At Akyab, in Burma, he handed over the mail to the crew of an Imperial Airways machine, and brought to Australia the second experimental airmail.

It could be done; there could be air links across the world. But when at this desperate time they begged for help from their government, there was none. Australian National Airways dwindled and died.

Now the team of crack pilots turned to giving joy flights from little country showgrounds to raise money. Kingsford Smith was never a man who cared greatly for money for itself; he was too generous. But failure!— that was different. For a national hero, giving showground rides was the equivalent of begging in the streets; and there were many good men doing just that in those times. But it hurt to land in a little bush town with the idea of scratching a few pounds together from the showground crowd; and to be met by the mayor and notables in a little procession, with their loud, stumbling praise and their welcome, their great honour of him. To the Australian people he was something a little more than human; he had a glow around him.

When Jim Mollison broke the solo record from Australia to England, the old, keen sense of triumph was sharp in the wind for Kingsford Smith. He was sure he could beat Mollison's flight record. He would cut a day here and a few hours in another place. He planned his course, and he readied the small plane, *Southern Cross Minor*, for a solo flight that would be like the flaring tail of a meteor across the world.

He *had* to do it again; go out on the old, long, monotonous, straining, sleepless air trail. It should be, compared with what he had done before—and how well he knew the track—just a milk run. If he came back breaking Mollison's record, surely he could beg a mail-carrying contract across the Tasman? He had to show that flying was safe and easy. Not just the little flight from the showground, but the long, steady passenger line. And the way to do it was to break the Australia-England record by himself.

Chapter Ten

THE AUSTRALIA-ENGLAND RUN

JAMES MOLLISON always brought out the worst in Australian airmen. He was, they considered, too fastidious. With his suede flying jacket and helmet, his suede shoes, he was altogether too well-groomed. But he was also in the front rank of world flyers. To beat his record of 8 days 21 hours from Australia to England would need skill, speed, and just that extra ounce of luck.

It was the luck that failed. Smithy had set off across Australia to Wyndham, the hopping-off port which had jinxed him once before. He had stopped at Alice Springs to repair the oil gauge pipe on the *Southern Cross Minor*, followed the Overland Telegraph line to Newcastle Waters, then struck west across the mulga country where Anderson and Hitchcock had died. His faith in Wyndham as a starting point was justified when, on the second afternoon, he passed Alor Star, halfway up the west coast of the Malay Peninsula. At Alor Star Mollison had spent his second night out from Darwin.

Then, eighty miles from Victoria Point, Kingsford Smith ran into a storm of blinding rain. To fly low was to run the risk of crashing into a hill. He had not enough petrol to fly blind out to sea. There was nothing else to do but land on the open beach which he could dimly see and spend the night in the pouring rain, with the tide washing around the plane's wheels.

The miserable dawn found him building a runway, single-handed, along the beach. He heard a tiger roar as he fell over himself, searching in the jungle for timber to lever up the wheels from the sucking wet sand.

The rain had stopped and the tide was going down. Just as a bush driver digs out a track when bogged on a western road, so Kingsford Smith dug out the sand and built tracks for each wheel facing the open sea. He made one start but the engine stopped. Two natives and their families came out of the jungle and watched the curious sight as he patiently dried out the magneto leads and petrol feeders. He jockeyed the plane into the air, and set off to Victoria Point, and then along the great stretch of coast to Rangoon.

But he was exhausted from the start and, by the time he was flying across the Bay of Bengal, he was ill indeed. He was vomiting and felt himself losing consciousness. He was tempted to pancake the *Southern Cross Minor* on the sea, sixty miles of it on either side, and just drift ashore. But he made Calcutta and, in furnace heat, he struggled over India, remembering to drop a note at Allahabad, apologising for not landing. He was now ahead of Mollison again, both at Allahabad and at Karachi. On the sixth day he was at Jask, at the mouth of the Persian Gulf, with 1,400 miles to fly to Aleppo on the Mediterranean.

A head-on sandstorm over the desert forced him to rise to 7,000 feet flying blind into a wind that slowed the plane down to fifty miles an hour. One night ahead of Mollison, he was content to be put to bed by the French mechanics at Aleppo, while they refuelled and over-hauled the *Southern Cross Minor*.

He intended to make Rome on the seventh day, but, sick and giddy, he was forced to land "more dead than alive" on a beach of Asia Minor in a Turkish military zone. A little crowd gathered around as he lay under the shadow of the plane's wing. The soldiery refused to let

him take off until permission came from Ankara, and a
night under guard quieted their suspicions.

Although Kingsford Smith freely expressed his opinion
of their ruining his chances, their stupidity probably saved
his life. He rested three days in Athens, abandoning the
attempt at the record, and from England returned to
Australia by sea.

The superstitious among his friends explained his
failure by pointing out that Nellie Stewart, whose photograph he had still faithfully carried on the flight, had died
while he was making it. Doctors diagnosed his illness as
poisoning by deadly carbon monoxide leaking from an

The natives watched the take-off.

exhaust pipe. He was still determined to prove that the
Australia-England run was safe, and profitable for a
regular air service.

The chance came the same year with the announcement of an official Christmas airmail to London. Australian National Airways was still carrying on, and the
Southern Sun was to make the flight with "Scotty" Allan
as pilot. But the *Sun*, laden with 45,000 letters and
packets, was unable to clear the waterlogged field at Alor
Star and crashed in a nearby rice field.

Kingsford Smith, with the company's chief engineer,
rushed off in the *Southern Star*. At Darwin they landed

in a heavy thunderstorm—it was the monsoon season—and on the sodden ground struck a telegraph post. Three days were spent in repairs and it was not until 5th December that they reached Alor Star and transferred the mail. It was now an old, familiar route: Calcutta, Karachi, Aleppo. Then snowstorms and fog dogged their flight, but when they reached Croydon, London on 16th December it was yet another record-breaking flight, thirteen and a half days.

In England, the imagination of people was stirred and a large New Year mail was assembled for Australia. The day before the *Southern Star* was ready to leave, the plane was damaged when Allan was forced to land, in dense fog, in a Kentish orchard. It was a week of repairs in freezing weather before they were ready. Gales delayed them, but, once started, they made Darwin in eleven days.

"We had demonstrated that, despite accidents, fogs, floods, wretched aerodromes and poor ground organisation, the Empire airmail service was a practical possibility." They had even made a profit.

But the Australian and English authorities were just not interested. So Smithy returned to giving rides at ten shillings a time on country showgrounds, with the added irony of being knighted Sir Charles Kingsford Smith while he was doing it.

It was, of course, a little embarrassing to the authorities that Smithy's "travelling circus" should be in Canberra, the Federal Capital, when the announcement was made. But Sir Isaac Isaacs, the first Australian Governor-General, saw no reason why the new knight should not spend the day giving joy flights in the Old Bus before attending the King's Birthday banquet at Government House.

For it was the *Southern Cross* that drew the people. To young and old it was a symbol like Nelson's *Victory*. To

fly in the *Southern Cross* was to have circled the earth.
At a little Queensland siding, Kingsford Smith took up
over four hundred people in one day. At least, he reflected,
with most of the planes laid up, he was making enough
to keep the business going.

By December 1932 they were ready to take the "travelling circus" to New Zealand. Kingsford Smith had with
him now a man who was to prove himself one of the
world's greatest navigators, Captain P. G. ("Bill") Taylor,
a master mariner turned airman. He had also a brilliant
journalist, Jack Percival, and John Stannage who had
married Kingsford Smith's niece.

The New Zealand tour was a great success, and they
returned to Australia after a "perfect" flight of thirteen
hours across the Tasman, convinced that a regular airmail
service to New Zealand, on which Kingsford Smith had
set his heart, was just within their grasp. By now he knew
that the Singapore-Australia stretch of the Empire air
route would never be given to him. Too many powerful
interests in British aviation were reserving it for themselves.

Still, he was determined to break that solo record. He
had left the *Southern Cross Minor* in England in 1931.
Two years later he went off to bring the plane back to
Australia, and, in spite of a return of his old illness for
the first half of the trip, he felt from Karachi onwards
that his old luck was returning. The little Percival Gull
could carry only 95 gallons of petrol and cruised along at
about 115 miles an hour. But he reached Wyndham in
7 days 4 hours and 45 minutes, completely shattering
James Mollison's record. In Melbourne, a crowd of 100,000
gathered to cheer him; and the Government made him a
grant of £3,000 which he sorely needed.

The year 1934 was the centenary of the State of Victoria.
There was to be a great new air race from England to

Australia—the MacRobertson Air Race with a prize of
£10,000. Kingsford Smith had been flying for seventeen
years. He was thirty-six. When Sir Ross and Sir Keith
Smith had won that first air race in 1919, he had been
kept out of it. If he could win this one—nobody knew the
route better, no one had flown it so often—he would wipe
out that terrible early disappointment.

And the Australian crowd believed he would do it.
He was the favourite, and they were backing him; their
hopes and their money were set on him.

But just as in that first air race everything had com-
bined against him, so it did now. He could not get the
British aircraft he wanted and had to order an American
one, a Lockheed Altair. This caused unfair comment,
though the best planes in Britain had been reserved for
British company pilots. "There was," wrote Kingsford
Smith, in reply to a newspaper's attack on him, "no other
British job comparable with the Comet."

Kingsford Smith had to buy a second-hand plane because of lack of money, but Lockheeds built him a new
wing and put in a new engine, though the repairs, as
it proved, were quite inadequate. But there were all
kinds of troubles over the registration. When it reached
Australia, the Customs officials refused to let it land until
the name *Anzac* was pasted over with paper, and Smithy
promised he would use another name. From Turkey came
the news that he must call personally at Ankara (Angora)
before he would be granted permission to fly over Asia
Minor. In Australia, officials kept up the irritating obstruc-
tions, the wooden, almost malicious hair-splitting of points
of etiquette.

There had been repair job after repair job every time
the Altair was tested out; and when, after a grim flight
in a Queensland duststorm, cracks appeared along the
cowling, "Bill" Taylor, at least, knew that Kingsford Smith

was out of the race. He could not get to the starting
aerodrome in England in time.

"So he wouldn't race against men who might beat him?"
the malicious whispered, in the bars and at the street
corners. "He couldn't face it! He had to shine alone or
he wouldn't try."

He knew he was out of favour with his backers, the
Australian people. The favourite who does not start is
always savagely abused. (As was Kingsford Smith.)

Charles Ulm, his old co-pilot, cabled offers of help from
America: "Tell Kingsford Smith I will obtain suitable
plane and fly it to England for him." But the *Lady
Southern Cross*, as the Altair was now called, had been
partly paid for by Smithy's friends.

Now he was out of the race he could only take the
plane back to the United States and sell it there. At
least, then his supporters would get their money back.
It was a single-engine machine and he would have to fly
east across the Pacific, a flight never before attempted.
But tufts of white feathers had been sent to his office.
He was down on the ground with a vengeance this time.

Still, it was to be a very different flight from that
desperate struggle, that first hit-or-miss meteor flare across
unknown perils when he had crossed from California,
with Ulm, and Warner and Lyons. In P. G. Taylor he knew
he had a navigator unequalled for skill and coolness;
and in the rebuilt *Lady Southern Cross* the fastest commercial plane in Australia.

When Kingsford Smith and Taylor brought the *Lady
Southern Cross* over San Francisco Bay after a record
fifteen-hours flight from Honolulu, it was "as spick and
span" as when they had set out from Brisbane.

Everything had been a miracle of neat pinpoint work.
A new genius of the air spaces had quietly meshed in
with the old. It was "Bill" Taylor in the cabin, with his

sextant, his chronometer, his sliding chart table and chart case, his pencils, his ball of marlin and half-crown torch in his little "box of treasures". In the cockpit, Smithy trusted Taylor implicitly, knew his worth, relied on his navigation. There was no photograph of Nellie Stewart, but as they left Brisbane a woman gave them a white rose "for luck".

The flight over the Pacific from west to east has been judged by aviation historians to be in many ways a greater flight than the first crossing; but while glory may be appetising, it is not nourishing. Kingsford Smith and Taylor left the *Lady Southern Cross* to be sold, while they shipped themselves home. At least, Smithy consoled himself, the old *Cross* still belonged to him. He could go on giving twelve-minute rides at fairgrounds.

Charles Ulm, too, was planning a Pacific flight, from America to Australia. He had the ambition to become the brains and direction of a great aviation company; but he had had to give up hope of ever doing that in Australia. He was "both a financial genius and a first-class airman" and planned to include New Zealand in his second crossing of the Pacific.

Somewhere off Hawaii, in December 1934, Ulm and his crew came down into the sea. The highly organised United States search failed to find even their bodies. The million-glittering waves took them, the ocean closed over them.

Chapter Eleven

THE FLAME FROM THE EXHAUST

"SMITHY STANDS on the wing replying to a volley of questions," wrote P. G. Taylor, at the end of the Pacific flight. "And pressed hard against the leading edge is a small American boy, trying hard to edge closer along the wing. I know what is happening to him. It happened to me when the *Southern Cross* flew over Pittwater in 1928. The spirit of adventure is surging within him, and he sees before him in wood and steel and human beings the material creation of the stories he has read."

Behind the figure of the great airman standing on the wing crouched the shadow of Big Business to whom Kingsford Smith was a spoilt child, a nuisance clamouring to be taken up when they were occupied with other affairs. They did not want him and his adventures, his loyal companions, his story-book bravery.

To set up a Trans-Tasman Air Service would need an outlay of £100,000; and Kingsford Smith could not even sell the *Lady Southern Cross* for what she had cost. He had to convince three governments, the Australian, the New Zealand, and, above all, the British, to whose views the Australian Government always deferred, that the Trans-Tasman service was profitable and safe.

The Kingsford Smith group, Jack Percival working hardest of all, had urged and begged until they had a promise of mail and goods to deliver in New Zealand. It became a joke among them that they might have to eat breakfast food or drink patent medicine on the flight;

advertisements might be all that would pay for the crossing of the Tasman.

Faith in Australia, which had belonged to the dead Ulm, was chartered to fly with the *Southern Cross*; but at the last, Kingsford Smith decided to take only the *Cross*. There was not enough payload for two aircraft. By that decision he probably saved the lives of two crews. *Faith in Australia* was unfit to fly; and Taylor was to have been her pilot.

Smithy stands on the wing.

But Taylor, exact and careful, was worried to see a dismantled engine from the *Southern Cross* lying on the hangar floor, while Percival and Stannage worked on it. Certainly the *Cross* had made the journey to New Zealand three times; they could not afford new planes until they made the flight. But—

"I am not an engineer," he wrote later, "and I have a strong dislike for pulling aeroplanes to pieces."

"Taking the *Cross*, Bill," Kingsford Smith had said. "Not enough mail to justify both machines."

"How about *Faith*? Her motors are in good condition, and she's in better shape right through."

"Nothing wrong with the *Cross*, Bill. Never let me down yet."

Taylor had a moment of anger; this faith in the *Southern Cross* was unreasonable. But it was not the engine of the *Southern Cross*, assembled by Percival and Stannage, which failed them but a small welding job to a new part, the manifold of the exhaust.

Nancy Bird that year, at the Kingsford Smith Flying School, became the youngest woman in the British Empire to obtain a commercial flyer's licence. She tells of the excitement as the *Southern Cross* set out on her last ocean flight. The *Cross* was not female to the Dutch who called it "The Father of the Fokkers"; but to Kingsford Smith "the *Cross*" was always "she".

"I had been at Richmond all day," writes Nancy Bird, "with the team from Mascot, and it was when Charles Kingsford Smith arrived in the late afternoon with P. G. Taylor and John Stannage, that one of the Air Force officials at the aerodrome came over, saying in the words of the regulation, 'No females may be present on His Majesty's Air Force stations after sundown.' The men backed me up. 'You keep out of the hangar and out of the lights,' they said. In the hours before the *Southern Cross* left I crouched in the shadow of her wings and drank the coffee the boys brought from the hangar."

Problems of maps, routes, weather, fuel loads, money and ways and means were now all left behind. In the small hours of the morning of 4th May 1935 the *Southern Cross* roared away, with the New Zealand Jubilee Mail and its load of merchandise.

As the night paled, Taylor found himself gazing fascinated at the flame from the centre exhaust, a jumping, flickering slit of light. The metal, weakened by heat, began to give and the crack expanded. The pipe broke, flicked out, and was gone in the airstream.

A convulsive shaking and smashing told that it had hit the starboard propeller. A spasm shook the *Southern Cross* as the metal pipe splintered the blade of the starboard motor. They fought to hold the height; and then, as the plane sank towards the sea, curve her back on a track towards the Australian coast.

The struggle now was not to reach New Zealand, but to save their lives if they could, to come down in the sea as near land as possible—land that was 600 miles away. They must rely on Kingsford Smith's ability to coax two motors to do the work of three.

Everything of weight had to go; first, the fuel. Taylor turned on the dump valves after calculating carefully that they must keep 300 gallons. Then they began to throw the cargo out the cabin door—women's hats for sale, their luggage, tools. "Anything except the mail," Kingsford Smith ordered. Even in their desperate situation he clung to the mail. Yet the slightest hair's-breadth of mistiming on his part and they would join the oddments hurtling down to the flat, wet, all-engulfing sea. What an end!

There were some nice technical problems with that broken propeller blade. If it began to revolve in the force of the sixty-five mile an hour airstream, the unbalanced blades set up a vibration that might wreck the whole plane. Kingsford Smith, when the broken propeller picked up speed, would set the *Southern Cross* almost on her tail until the propeller stopped moving. As he did so, the *Cross* would sink towards the sea. Not many planes could have taken this. Levelling out, under his control, the *Cross* sagged on again. If, thought Taylor, the blades could be trimmed, they might get some thrust from it. He tried to cut off the shattered blade with a hacksaw, but any pressure started the propeller turning in the windblast.

They had been struggling for five hours—330 miles still to go—when the blue smoke from the port exhaust began to trouble Taylor more than the immediate danger of drowning. The port engine was burning oil; only to be expected when it was overtaxed. But how long could they go on with it burning oil? There was oil in the tank behind the useless starboard motor. The needle on the pressure gauge for the port engine fell lower and lower. Down below the wrinkled sea crawled like a scaled monster.

"Going to have a stab at getting some oil," Taylor shouted to Smithy. The pilot shook his head. Taylor, with his coat belted tightly, in his stockinged feet, lashed a light line from the mailbags, one end to his middle, one to a steel tube in the cockpit. It would be about as useful as a cobweb if he fell, but it made him feel better.

He had one leg over the side, feeling with his toes for the pipeline from the motor to the fuselage. The airstream grabbed at him, screamed, flattened the breath in his mouth, flattening his eyelids so that he could not look up. He began, in the gulf of his own terror, to edge his feet slowly along the strut, the rigid edge of the wing behind his neck, shuffling along inch by inch to reach the engine mounting. When he reached it the thought of being stuck out there alone was worse. And how was he to get the oil drain plug from the side of the cowl? A spanner; had they thrown them all out? Stannage understood, and had the spanner ready, as he slowly shifted across to reach it, holding on to the strut with one hand. Their hands just met.

"I climb down to a position straddling and sitting on this horizontal strut, hook my left arm around the tube and thus have available both hands to wangle the spanner into position and tighten it on the head of the drain plug."

What would he put the oil in? Taylor had reached the stage now of thinking reasonably. Stannage waited with a thermos flask. Taylor slid along again, passed the spanner through a cautious eternity, took the flask; left arm round the tube, one hand to unscrew the plug, one to jam the flask against the bottom of the tank when the loosened plug came out. Try doing it in a hurricane. And the plug must be put in again. It must.

He had only one hand now to help in the shuffle back. The other held the oil, much of it whipped away by the windstream as the flask passed from the shelter of Taylor's body. Stannage had a small suitcase ready.

Next time—what next time?—Taylor would squeeze the top of the thermos flask so less oil was lost. Incredibly, they kept on passing the thermos, taking oil to the suitcase.

Now there was the struggle to put the oil in the engine on the other side of the cockpit. Climbing over Smithy as he piloted the *Southern Cross*, Taylor forced his body out against the blast, struggling to reach the port tank; against the airstream it seemed impossible. But Kingsford Smith had thought of another of his brilliant piloting devices. He turned off the port motor so that the blast was lessened. The plane lost height rapidly; but Taylor was safely hugging the struts, as Smithy lifted the *Southern Cross* again, almost from the sea.

At full throttle now the port motor sent a great torrent of air beating like a waterfall, crushing Taylor against the

He edged along the strut.

engine mounting. The sound of the engine a few inches from his ear was deafening. Again the port motor was shut off, and the perilous transfer of oil was made.

Half an hour later it had all to be done again; six times before they could expect to see land. Now they had worked out a system: Stannage ready; Kingsford Smith ready to shut off the port motor, and then to fight for height when Taylor was clinging to the strut.

Taylor was out there, battered in the stream of air, when they threw out the Jubilee Mail. The bitter problem had become easy and simple. You have a man risking his life; you have weight. Out goes the weight. The man comes shuffling in inch by inch, holding the thermos against his stained jacket. Only the lightness of the load keeps the plane flying.

About thirty miles from land, Taylor, now certain of success, made the last oil change that would bring the plane into Mascot aerodrome. Kingsford Smith was against his doing it again, but when the laborious business was all gone through they were over the coast.

The *Cross* came in to her hangar after nine hours of such flying as no man who had not Kingsford Smith's iron endurance could have sustained.

That night he nearly drowned in his bath. His wife found him sleeping peacefully with his nose just above the water.

P. G. Taylor was awarded the Empire Gallantry Medal, later to be replaced by the George Cross.

Chapter Twelve

TO BE A HERO IS NOT ENOUGH

KINGSFORD SMITH decided that he would take the *Lady Southern Cross* to England and try to sell the Lockheed Altair there. He could not sell it in America. She needed a certificate from the international aviation authorities that would give her a more useful commercial range. The troubles over that plane's registration had been ever present.

At thirty-eight years of age, Kingsford Smith had pushed himself harder than any man alive. Always before a long flight he trained like a fighter. But, in England, he was nibbled at by Business. He had never been a business man. All his life he seemed to have been trying to persuade officials, and now he was having no success. He could *not* sell the *Lady Southern Cross*.

The news from Australia of his company was desperate, and he was impatient to be back as soon as he could. He wasn't so much afraid about the money; so often before he had been broke. Something would lift him up again. He just wanted to be in the air. Thirty-eight! And how long could he keep going?

He had sworn never to strain on a record flight again; but he needed to get home fast. A record-breaking flight to Australia was the answer. It didn't matter that he had influenza. What about the time he recovered from an appendix operation to fly to Australia? So he argued with himself.

Before he had left Australia he had sold the *Southern*

Cross, one of his last personal belongings, to the Australian Government. The *Cross* was worth to him at least £10,000. The Government tried to beat him down to £1,500; for a far less famous aeroplane the American Government had paid four times that amount. Finally, the Australian Government got the *Southern Cross* for the promise of £3,000.

In the ceremony when Kingsford Smith handed over his plane, the Minister for Defence said that he accepted "this most famous aeroplane from the man whose magnificent airmanship had made history in Australia". He declared: "Sir Charles has my assurance that it will remain here at Richmond only as long as it takes to provide appropriate accommodation for it at the Federal Capital."

For twenty-one years the *Southern Cross* was hidden away. Dismantled, it was shifted from one hangar to another as space was grudged for its existence. The Treasury could spare no money for its housing, and it was dumped in the dark corner of a store.

In England, Kingsford Smith thought he had at least £3,000 in cash in Australia; until, when he was running short, he asked that £300 be sent to him. Not only had the Commonwealth Treasury *not* paid for the *Southern Cross*; it was raising all kinds of questions as to whether he even owned the *Cross*. She had been a free gift from the American, Captain G. Allan Hancock, to Kingsford Smith and Charles Ulm. When Ulm decided to leave Australia, he had accepted shares in Australian National Airways in place of his half interest. Five months after Kingsford Smith was dead, a cheque was sent to his widow.

For the record-breaking attempt, some genius of red tape in England decreed that the *Lady Southern Cross*, which had carried a load of 520 gallons of petrol on the flight across the Pacific, should now take only 118 gallons. Kingsford Smith was ill and exhausted; but just to get into the air, to break that last record, would put him on top again.

He had Tommy Pethybridge, competent in everything, for his companion. By the time they were leaving Allahabad they knew they were only four hours behind the record set in the Centenary Air Race. If they flew non-stop to Singapore, they would more than make up those four hours.

In the night, above the Gulf of Martaban, James Melrose who was himself flying to Australia, saw the flare of a plane's exhaust. It could only be that of the *Lady Southern Cross* tearing the darkness apart on her doomed journey.

They must have struck the trees.

Two years later, part of the undercarriage was found off that Burma coast. And in the fringe of coastal islands was one where trees had been ripped down, a furrow of disaster, from the crest of a high hill. In the pitch-black night, just a little too low, they must have struck those trees; and the broken plane plunged into the sea beyond. The bodies of Sir Charles Kingsford Smith and T. E. Pethybridge were never recovered.

The New Zealander, Clouston, flying to Australia in 1938, looked down at dusk on the dried, weather-broken rocks of the Andaman Islands, and shouted dramatically to his companion: "Down there on the ocean bed is presumed to be the body of Kingsford Smith and the *Southern Cross*."

He was wrong, of course. The *Southern Cross's* body had survived, bought by those who had once held her master high, tossed him down, praised him as their darling, refused him help, lifted him up again.

He had staggered on until his strength gave out, always trying, sometimes succeeding, in efforts too great. He was a hero, of course, sober people said; but hadn't he been always too gay, too gallant, almost vulgarly so? And it was fitting, wasn't it, that he should die like that?

He would trouble them no more. The great airliners he had never been allowed to own, or to run, could now soar above him, managed on methodical lines, with proper time sheets and reasonable man hours.

There is a neat, warm, sealed compartment of everyday life. Outside it stretches unfathomably the roaring darkness; and there, with danger as one of their crew, will always ride the men who, like Kingsford Smith, conquer space and time, shining in their gaiety and their doom.

Chapter Thirteen

A MAN IS SAFE WITH THE STARS
FOR FRIENDS

THE ONE THOUGHT in the minds of his friends was that Smithy was lost and they had to find him. Harry Purvis, John Stannage and Gordon Taylor set off in a small twin-engine plane; Taylor exhausted with worry and lack of sleep.

In Cloncurry he went to the doctor of the Department of Civil Aviation, to ask for something to keep him going. He could not sleep, he had to go on to Darwin, he explained; the aircraft was waiting. The doctor told him he was not fit to fly; he must have "complete rest". Taylor had not been affected before by his nightmare climb on the wings of the *Southern Cross* above the Tasman Sea; but now, just when he wanted to be at his best, the delayed shock had crept up on him.

Before he gave in to the doctor he took the plane up to prove to himself that he could fly again. He tested it and himself in the air, flinging it about in loops and turns. He had not liked the way it behaved on the trip up from Sydney. Harry Purvis, piloting it back, managed to land safely on a claypan where he found the aileron cable was loose. If they had gone on, there would probably have been another fatal crash.

Taylor felt utterly dejected, a last survivor of the old group of flyers, the missing link. Ulm was dead; Kingsford Smith was dead, killed, Taylor thought bitterly, by the jungle warfare for the possession of the air trails they had blazed. He himself had been flying for nearly twenty years. When he looked around he saw that most of the men who had flown with him were dead or finished, retired. The doctors felt he should get a job on the ground.

Taylor believed that he needed to fly and that he must fly. In his slim little Gull aircraft he was soon in the air again on important charter flights, bringing pictures of far-off events for the newspaper for which Jack Percival was working. It was hard flying, but the kind of invigorating action Taylor needed.

There were still great flights to be made, new routes to be opened up, and Taylor planned, coolly, methodically. He interested the Australian Government in the importance of an air route from Australia across the Indian Ocean to Africa. Against all opposition and delay he carried through the complicated preparations for the first flight. Searching for a suitable plane in England, he heard of one in New Guinea, and managed to charter the *Guba*, a Catalina flying boat, before he had any promise of official support.

The Australian and British governments then took over the charter and commissioned him to lead the flight across the Indian Ocean, from Port Hedland (W.A.) to Kenya.

Taylor was a thinking man, a writer. He had been a flight commander in the First World War, and at that time a passion seized him to turn flying to peaceful ends. He loved water and had been bred beside it, sailing a small boat as a relief from school, loving the trees of the bush, the birds and animals. After the war he had owned an amphibian plane, and would land in peaceful coves up and down the east coast of Australia, from the north to Tasmania.

In those early years he had wanted to be able to come down on water at night, and so he worked out a kind of rod which would flick the waves and register the descent of the plane. A sea captain had first shown him the constellations of the southern heavens, and with his tables of calculations he could work out the problems of navigation. The stars were his friends and guides, familiar as the lamps on suburban streets.

Taylor would always be exact and thoughtful. He knew the unknown airway to Africa would tax his skill in navigation to the limit. He had to find the Cocos Islands, and survey the other islands of the Indian Ocean which might be useful if, as seemed likely, war broke out and the air route to England was cut.

He needed the friendly stars on this flight to Africa, and they were clear in the sky when the *Guba* left Port Hedland. The *Guba* went up in the light of the setting sun, and a good star fix kept it flying steadily for the Cocos Islands. Soon, the dark clouds, the wind and the rain sent them higher, trying to clear the storms and lightning. Without the stars, when he has no radio, a navigator's tools are useless; and there were no radio guides over that black ocean, no radar.

Taylor had with him the *Guba's* navigator. They had plotted their course with all care. They could not, in the stormy weather, find the Cocos Islands. Groping through the rain and wind Taylor was faced with a bitter decision. He must fly to Java before their emergency fuel gave out. He would not risk the lives of the crew.

They were lucky enough to have one glimpse of the sun which allowed them to set a course for Batavia (Djakarta). At Batavia, they rested and then started out again. Once more they made their way through storms, taking drift sights on the sea and keeping their compass course. This time they succeeded in locating Cocos.

They landed in a peaceful lagoon to be met by the islanders whose happy world would never be the same again. From Cocos they flew with brilliant stars for Diego

Garcia in the Chagos group, and spent a week of careful survey, planning and mapping for the men who would come after them. Again in the Seychelles Islands they did the same thing, arriving at last in Mombasa, the island port of Kenya.

Taylor's report on his return gave the Royal Navy and the Royal Air Force the information and the bases they needed against raiding submarines in the Indian Ocean. When war broke out, and Japan cut the air route via Singapore, a new way through the Cocos Islands was opened between Perth in Western Australia and Colombo.

It was a secret route, and one American, perplexed by the movements of the Australians and their planes, asked what it was all about. "We just take the plane round that headland," a casual Australian explained, "and sell the petrol on the black market." The Colombo route was a lifeline in the desperate years when the Japanese held Singapore and the Dutch East Indies. It came as a result of Taylor's flight. After the war a regular service was begun to Africa.

Taylor, during the Second World War, was again faced with the problem that people would think he was too old, and would try to keep him on the ground. But he was a persistent man, and met danger and the stars again, flying planes from Canada to England across the North Atlantic. All the time he was planning for another great flight. He had to wait until the war in Europe was, in 1944, nearing its last stages before he could urge his scheme for a route via Mexico to Clipperton Island in the Pacific and so across the Central Pacific by a chain of islands to Australia.

It needed all the enormous patience, the detailed arguments of which Taylor was a master, to convince the three governments of the usefulness of this scheme. He had to deal in international politics, for what he was proposing was a British-Australian venture; and the United States was controlling the war in the Pacific. Not until he had fought his way through officials and red tape to President Roosevelt, did the men who were hindering him give way. The President gave orders that the Australian was to be helped to make the flight.

Even when he was in the air over Mexico Taylor was uncertain whether, at the last moment, he would be allowed to go on. The question was raised as to who really owned the patch of coral with a lagoon that was Clipperton Island. Taylor comforted himself with the thought that all the long-distance pioneers had found their most wearisome troubles beset them in the effort to get away. Once you set out there was only clean danger instead of a web of hindrances.

When he was a boy it had been Lion Island, at the entrance to Broken Bay, that he had set his little sailboat to explore. Before the war it had been far-off Cocos Island to which his flight was set. Now it was this strange Clipperton Island, about which so little was known, that drew him on. There had been a lighthouse there, now in ruins, the scene of murder and tragedy. The survivors had left when they were in danger of starving to death. For years the island had been lost, almost unknown.

Taylor would need first to fly out with a load of fuel, to find out if the coral made the lagoon too dangerous for landing. He would leave the fuel, come back for more and then make Clipperton his base to launch out on the long stages across the Pacific.

For this survey flight he had another Catalina; he always approved of planes that could land on water for these survey flights. He called her *Frigate Bird*, from the great-winged seabirds to which the natives of the Cocos Islands had likened the plane in which he navigated the Indian Ocean. He took gifts for natives he might meet, two rubber dinghys, anchors, fishing gear and provisions for an emergency.

Always with the great loads of petrol needed for these long-distance flights the problem was what had to be left behind. For Taylor, the unimportant things were the heavy metal parts of seats, iron for show rather than for strength. They must have concentrated food, water tanks, tablets for making salt water drinkable, spare parts.

He had a New Zealander, Henderson, as navigator. Henderson knew the Pacific Islands and was a good man with boats. "Navigators are sometimes described as temperamental," said Taylor, "because they object to having cans of baked beans opened on their clean charts, and to having people use their dividers to stab open a can of condensed milk. Navigators and radio operators live in a trance," he claimed. "They just don't like anybody breaking into it."

The radio man, Len Bligh, came from a sheep station in Australia and was a descendant of the famous Captain Bligh of the *Bounty*, the great Pacific seaman. The engineer, Jock Hogg, was to have a terrible time trying to make repairs in desperate conditions. His was the heart-breaking task.

The lagoon at Clipperton Island was a dangerous landing place, but Taylor successfully, almost miraculously, brought the overloaded *Frigate Bird* through the coral that would have ripped the thin duralumin of the flying boat to pieces if there had been one false move. They paddled ashore in the dinghy and set up a Robinson Crusoe-like camp while they laid out tanks on the beach and pumped fuel into them through a long hosepipe. They explored the island with its traces of forgotten dead, the rock burrowed by dark tunnels where wild pig lurked.

With the fuel base set up they could return to Mexico,

and on the second visit to Clipperton they had at least
the advantage of knowing how treacherous were the chan-
nels through the coral lagoon. The weather was now
worse, but they set up camp, a new and better one with a
table in a lean-to shelter. They could live there on fish
and pig if they had to. And when the engineer, Jock
Hogg, found he had not the tools he needed, they blessed
the radio that allowed them to ask for their relief plane
to fly out special parts for the damaged engine.

It was a nightmare island for Jock Hogg. On a tiny
atoll he found *Frigate Bird* needed a new cylinder. The
plugs had jammed in and one was broken. For such a
job he needed a well-equipped workshop. But the parts
were to be flown out.

Taylor wondered how, when their survey was complete,
he would get the *Frigate Bird* into the air again. The
lagoon was two miles long, but it had a great reef across
it, and the most he could hope for was a take-off a mile
long which was not enough for a heavily loaded flying
boat. While he was racking his brains and Hogg was
trying to loosen the engine nuts in the hot sun, the relief
plane arrived. Hogg hammered out a special tool which
he made on an old anvil in the ruins of a blacksmith's
shop. But even this and a blowtorch could not move the
plug.

Now, the weather closed in on the two crews. Their
first anxiety was for the planes in danger of being blown
from their anchors. When they realised that a hurricane
was upon them, and as the camp simply blew away, it
became a question not only of whether they could save
the two aircraft but their lives. The men were flattened
to the ground by gusts from the hundred mile an hour
hurricane. The sea swept in waves across the island.

The moorings for the *Frigate Bird* had been made with
incredible labour: a mass of old ship's chains and rusty

iron. The relief plane had no such moorings, but there for seven hours Hicks, the pilot, sat at the controls lifting the engines against the force of the hurricane, in a mountain of foam through which the water showed no surface.

There was only one place of comparative safety on the island, a group of palms in the shelter of the rock which rose above the flat coral ground. Stumbling and falling the rest of the crew made their way there, almost reconciled to the thought that Hicks and the flying boats were lost.

The hurricane was upon them.

In an interval of the storm Taylor set out in the little rubber dinghy allowing it to be blown towards the *Frigate Bird* whose two engines were out of action. But the moorings had held, even the fuel raft was safe; and, on the relief plane, Hicks still kept the engines at steady speed against the wind.

After the hurricane came the hair-raising take-off and the flight of 3,000 miles to Bora Bora, a distance equal to that of London to New York. The survey had shown that with the blasting of certain great masses of coral reef, the lagoon could be made safe for regular landings by flying boats. But to take off with the *Frigate Bird's* heavy load of petrol was a masterpiece of technique.

On the long flight Taylor nursed his engines to increase the cruising range worked out, partly by intricate curves and graphs, and partly by his judgement of the way the plane behaved. He liked to let his mind dwell on delicate mathematical problems of speed and fuel consumption and engine performance.

"The navigator, living with the stars, a chart, instruments and books of tables, all of which are concrete things, and inhabiting a lighted cabin, is often less aware of the possibility of error than the pilot alone out in the night." On long ocean flights, Taylor knew, the pilot was liable to let the plane wander a little, but usually his errors fell in a regular pattern. A wise navigator soon learnt this and took it into consideration when he made out the compass course.

The navigation was, of course, without the aid of radio. It was checked by taking double drift flares dropped from the tunnel hatch, for they used the wind when they could find it, as the old sailing ships had done. Taking the flame float from the rack, pulling the pin, dropping it through the roar of the open tunnel hatch, they watched for the light to flicker on the sea; and with that point sighted, the navigator worked, measuring the wind and direction.

So they pitted sheer brain power, will and nerve and resource against the powers of darkness; and came first to the rock in the ocean which was their target, then to the bright green islands, the low coasts of coral, and at last to Bora Bora, where the *Frigate Bird* could be checked.

While they were taxi-ing for the take-off they discovered water in the tanks. Seventeen hundred gallons of fuel had to be drained; the tanks dried out. But they had *checked*; they had found out before they started.

They left for the Tuamotos, "a drift sight job", seeking an atoll 570 miles away. They surveyed Tahiti from the air as a base for land and sea aircraft, as they had searched the Marquesas for possible bases. They were not breaking records; this was the scouting and exploring expedition which made possible the great tourist traffic of today to the once peaceful islands of the Pacific.

They went on to New Zealand, and when the *Frigate Bird* arrived she had 10,000 miles of ocean flight behind her. If ever a flight was faultless it was this one. Taylor just flew the *Frigate Bird* back to America by the more conventional route, across the United States to Fort Worth and then to her base in the Bermuda Islands.

He had had a vision of the new route as a great feat of English, Australian and New Zealand co-operation. In London, it had been treated as a plot to disrupt the British Empire. He returned to find Dakotas ready in Canada to begin the task of preparing a base on Clipperton Island; but while they were still grounded the United States took possession and warned off all other nations. In 1965, twenty years after Taylor's flight, Qantas established the new Mexico service over his route.

When Taylor had made the first west-east crossing of the Pacific with Kingsford Smith in the *Lady Southern Cross*, he had examined the islands from the air and suggested places suitable for British air bases. The United States built the bases when England showed no interest.

Taylor was willing to let governments and airlines fight it out for themselves. He liked the island peoples and detested the thought that they must be spoiled by tourism and by cities of hotels rising on their shores. But machine living would come in any case, and he felt that his was only the task of opening the great crossings over oceans where there had been none before.

Chapter Fourteen

ABOUT A THOUSAND MILES.
A LITTLE OUT OF
GLIDING DISTANCE FROM LAND

EVERY MAN in an aircraft has what Gordon Taylor calls his "personal magic" that comforts him: the mascot that must sit in a certain place, his own cushion or pencil. He sets about establishing a little corner which is his own. Even in a motor car, a prison cell or a hospital ward, a human being will establish his identity, if only by moving a matchbox a little to the left.

After World War II, humanity was like a disturbed ant heap, with whole populations homeless, on the move, brimming out from the old cities that had been destroyed. Taylor was convinced that there would be a great flow of people to warmer countries, like Australia and South America, with more hope, they thought, for the future. He believed Australia and, to a lesser extent, South America, would probably face settlement on a scale which they had not experienced before. It was important that the enormous distances of ocean which lay between Australia and South America should be bridged by air. No one had ever faced the flight from eastern Australia to Chile, but he intended to make it.

This would be the last and most difficult trans-ocean flight. Could it be done? Over the Southern Ocean, the bright and tiny islands ruled by France were scattered across French Oceania. He would go by known ways to Noumea, Suva, Samoa, Aitutaki, Tahiti. But in 1950 there was no known passage for aircraft east of Tahiti; and this alone was more than 4,000 nautical miles to the coast of Chile—farther than across the North Pacific from Vancouver to Yokohama. No seaplane could carry such a load of fuel.

If he had a small ship to take aviation fuel to the far-off island of Mangareva, he could use that fuel to cross the 1,400 miles to Easter Island, where the stone faces of forgotten gods stared out of the grass to the sea. He must have more fuel at Easter Island, for between it and South America lay 2,000 miles of water. And at Easter Island there was no sheltered lagoon or harbour for a plane.

People said he was mad to think that a flying boat could take off from the open sea. But there must be a way. Just before he left he hit on the idea of rockets. He tested them out in the Catalina which the Australian Government had given him for the flight, and they worked well, thrusting the plane up out of the water. But it was carrying only a light load. How would it work with a load of petrol for 2,000 miles?

His good friend Group Captain Thomas White was now Minister for Aviation, and with an old flyer like White ready to cut all the red tape and assist him, the customary weary arguments with men whose job was to frame restrictions, were all smoothed out in advance.

Not until Taylor had named his Catalina *Frigate Bird II* did he learn of the sinister legend of Easter Island that this was where the frigate bird, the Manutara, came to lay its egg and die. Two months before *Frigate Bird II* set off from Rose Bay, in Sydney Harbour, a Chilean plane called the *Manutara* had landed at Easter Island. It had broken a wing trying to get off and the plane was still there. Always the first men to go out on a new way must face some element of the unknown.

Taylor had been flying thirty-five years; he was the

veteran of them all. He had survived—and if he did not survive—well, it would be worth it. He had a crew of old friends, men who had flown with him on airlines or on the great ocean explorations. Captain Harry Purvis would be his first officer; and the indomitable Jack Percival came as official correspondent.

Jack Percival had learnt resource in many plane flights, in theatres of war, in the Philippines, and as a prisoner-of-war of the Japanese. He had come from Korea to join this flight; yet he cheerfully volunteered to do the cooking.

Taylor's two small daughters came to see their father off. "They knew what the score was. They knew how you found an island, and what sort of place you needed for shelter when you arrived." His wife had died, but they were good, brave children. If something went wrong— but it had to be accepted! He thought of the anchors, for the hurricane at Clipperton Island had taught him the value of anchors for holding a flying boat in a storm. He surveyed his chart table with the waterproof cover over his clean charts ("All Catalinas leak water through the roof hatch"); his pencil sharpener "just so" on the edge of the table. These were Taylor's personal magic, his sextants, his maps, his calculations to aid his will and brain against chaos.

All the way to Noumea, to Suva, Samoa, Tahiti, there stayed, like a small cloud at the back of his mind, Easter Island, that triangular island of dead volcanoes and great cliffs where the lone frigate bird, Manutara, came to die. Then the dangerous landing in the coral of the lagoon at Aitutaki was over, and they were met at Mangareva by the French ship *Tamara*, which had once towed the Kon Tiki. It had brought their fuel.

At Mangareva they fitted the rockets. They had a scare when *Frigate Bird II* snapped her anchor by night and would have drifted on the coral, had not the engineer who was on board started the engines and brought her off. There was no wind; the cable must have been faulty. Luckily they had found out, before their lives depended on that cable. Starting "cold"—without first turning the engines over—could have damaged them, but it did not seem to have done so.

It was not luck, but care, that saved them the third time when, testing every drum of fuel before it went into the tanks, they found a drum of diesel oil had been included among them from the ship. Had that gone into the tanks . . .

The weather report from Easter Island was favourable, and they flew by night to take advantage of the stars. They would need a long, smooth take-off from Easter Island. All they wanted there was just two hours, time enough to load in the aviation fuel.

They were worn out by lack of sleep; the radio was not bringing anything in; but Easter Island, a faint dark patch, showed straight ahead from the star navigation. They circled the village above the cliffs trying to make radio contact. They could see a mooring buoy and a small boat basin, but the wind was smashing a great swell up the cliffs there.

If they landed on the other side of the island, it would shelter them from the force of the wind. There was nothing else to do. In one lane between the rocks, where the plane could edge up under the cliffs, there was a small patch of sand for the anchors. Here they came to rest. The stainless steel of the anchor slid down and bit in, and the rope tightened.

People were climbing down the cliffs, and a man swam out bringing a carved, wooden sword in the shape of a frigate bird; on the hilt was *Manutara.*

Soon ten other men swam out. A motor boat approached but it did not have their fuel. In that leisurely island nobody seemed to realise their desperate case. Taylor, Percival and Purvis went ashore to see what could be done. The petrol would have to be brought round six miles, and nobody had made any preparations except for a feast, a day of welcome.

They arranged that Harry Purvis would stay at the little stone dock to keep the fuel moving. Taylor, observing the weather, was taken back to the boat landing by

A man swam out bringing a carved wooden sword.

jeep. There was cloud building up to the south. By three in the afternoon the pipes were connected and the tanks of *Frigate Bird* were filling from the drums in the old whaleboats alongside, but the rising seas sent the boats clanging against the aircraft.

Frigate Bird must try for a take-off before dark; but it was too late. When they cautiously pushed her out into the swell, the water breaking over her propellers sent her staggering. Rain and black night were closing down; breakers boomed in against the cliffs.

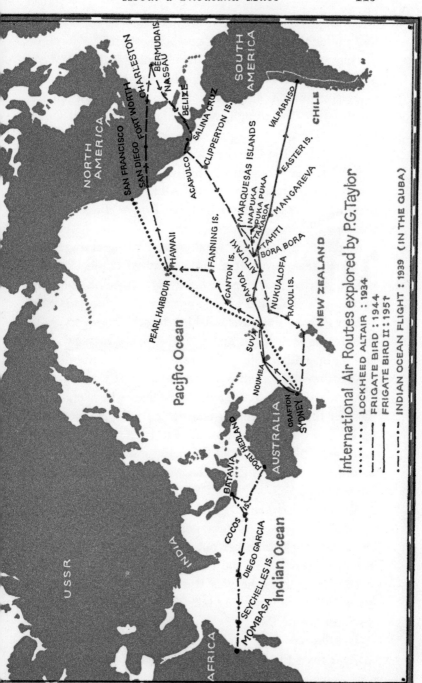

International Air Routes explored by P.G.Taylor

⋯⋯⋯⋯ LOCKHEED ALTAIR : 1934
– – – – – FRIGATE BIRD : 1944
――――― FRIGATE BIRD II : 1951
–·–·–·– INDIAN OCEAN FLIGHT : 1939 (IN THE GUBA)

Taylor decided he would anchor close to rocks a few feet under the surface of a bombora where the force of the seas would be broken by the churning water just clear of the surf. A touch, a whisker, and she would be smashed to pieces; but the anchors took her, and she rose on the swell, fell in the trough, with a clang of the hull and a smack of the tail.

They asked the islanders in the whaleboat for another anchor. It was brought, and in the rain and darkness, the boat stood by ready to rescue, calling through the night a signal to those on land that the *Frigate Bird* was still there.

At dawn, the faithful whaleboat, beating through tremendous seas, brought a radio message telling the best time to arrive in Chile—as far away as Melbourne from Perth—for the officials to welcome them at Quinteros base!

The *Frigate Bird* was crashing to and fro, every wave threatening to tear her apart. Taylor, more than two days and nights without sleep, felt a surge of anger and despair. Unless they did something soon the aircraft would be lost.

A little cushion that Taylor cherished was keeping out most of the water from a hole in the perspex. Now they had to start the engines running to breast the big swells. Little by little they edged the plane away from the rocks to open sea, pumping out the water with an emergency hand pump.

Taylor *sailed* the *Frigate Bird* as he once sailed an open boat. He had to take her out to sea, let the wind drive her back, take her out again, working his way up the coast and round the corner of the island. Trying to clear the anchors, he was washed off the plane, nearly pounded by the smacking tail. They managed to haul him back on a rope.

Drifting on their sailing tack, they jettisoned fuel, in danger from the fumes if they started the engine. Pumping and bailing, they rounded South Cape and sailed with the roar and foam of surf behind them. There was smooth water two miles ahead and they could take on more fuel. But they must go immediately, for the *Frigate Bird* had been given a dangerous beating.

At five o'clock there were still 200 gallons to be pumped; and then they were ready. The way the sea ran now, they must take the plane out to sea. All would depend on the rockets. If the rockets failed, the *Frigate Bird's* bottom would disintegrate as she hit the water. But the rockets worked!

When they reached that great welcome in Chile, Taylor was faced with a hard decision. There had been plans for a goodwill flight of the *Frigate Bird* over South America; but their nightmare stay at Easter Island meant that this important stopping place might be blacklisted by the regulation framers. "Look at what happened to Taylor," they would say. "Easter Island can't even be considered." He went back. He would fly the Pacific once again. He would defeat Easter Island, that deathplace of seabirds.

Again Easter Island threatened them with wind and seas. It was eight hours before the fuel was brought by the boats. In panting, gasping desperation they filled the tanks at last. There were cloud and rain and surf, with just the base of the cliffs showing as they made their roaring run; but again they were out safe into the squalls and storms, nosing for the clear stars.

The port float would not lock up, but they wound it up by hand and lashed it. Nothing could stop them now.

When they reached Suva, Taylor circled low over Naselei Beach, a salute to his old comrade, Kingsford Smith. How many years was it since the two of them had taken off from Naselei for Honolulu? Friends do not forget.

Frigate Bird II came home, down the coast of Australia to her base at Rose Bay in Sydney Harbour. Behind them lay the storms, the long nights without sleep, the refuelling at Mangareva from drums left under the coconut palms by the *Tamara*, in which they had been helped by friendly islanders in outrigger canoes.

Gordon Taylor brought *Frigate Bird II* into her base at exactly three o'clock as the second hand touched. Planes must always run exactly on time, he thought.

But there was more to it than that. In the ringing silence of the sky, man seeing the fair curves of earth in a garment of light, was aware of the lonely secrets of life. There, above the struggling and the scheming, the last ray of sunlight was the will of God, a knifeblade at his throat, his plane a dustmote in the glance of heaven; and the blue parchment of the sky unrolled for some awesome consultation in which men, too, were they daring enough, had some participation.

THE TRAILS THEY BLAZED

Lawrence Hargrave:

For twenty-five years, from 1884 to 1909, Lawrence Hargrave experimented with box-kites and monoplane models. At Stanwell Park, N.S.W., in 1894 he raised himself 16 feet by an arrangement of box-kites against a 21 m.p.h. wind. The first aeroplane ever to fly publicly, that of Santos Dumont, in France, 1906, was a development of Hargrave's box-kites, as were all the early biplanes such as the Voison.

Hargrave invented the rotary engine and built models driven by 3-cylinder engines. Early aircraft engines such as the Gnome, Clerget and Le Rohone, were based on his gas turbine engine.

He refused to patent any of his inventions. "Knowledge should be free."

Harry Houdini:

Houdini made the first flights in Australia in a powered aircraft, a Voison, on 18th March 1910.

John Duigan, M.C.:

Duigan built a biplane on his father's sheep station in 1910. It was built of red pine and ash wood, steel bands off wool bales and piano wires. From July to September 1910 he made 27 flights in this, the first Australian-made aeroplane. He flew with the Australian Flying Squadron No. 3.

William Ewart Hart:

"Bill" Hart was the first pilot licensed in Australia. When the Bristol Aircraft Company refused to teach Hart to fly its box-kite, unless he agreed not to build aircraft in Australia, Hart taught himself. He made the first cross-country flight of 40 miles, from Penrith to the Sydney Cricket Ground, reaching a height of 6,500 feet. His machine flew at 55 m.p.h. or not at all! Hart made many reckless flights until a final crash broke many bones. In the Middle East he continued to train pilots for No. 1 Squadron of the Australian Flying Corps.

The first four pilots at the R.A.A.F. mother base at Point Cook, Victoria, were:

T. W. White, later Sir Thomas White, D.F.C., Minister for Air, and Australian High Commissioner in London;
Richard Williams, later first Australian Air Marshall, Sir Richard Williams, later first Australian Air Marshal, Sir at the age of 31;
Lieutenant G. P. Merz, killed in action, 1915;
Captain D. T. W. Manwell.

Sir Ross Macpherson Smith, K.B.E., M.C. and Bar, D.F.C. and 2 Bars; and Sir Keith Macpherson Smith, K.B.E., flew the first England-Australia flight, 1919, in a Vickers-Vimy aircraft, in 28 days: the G-EAOU—"God 'Elp All Of Us".

Raymond Parer, A.F.C. and J. C. McIntosh flew from England to Australia, 1920. Later Raymond Parer operated New Guinea Transport Services.

Chief flights of Squadron Leader Herbert John Louis Hinkler, A.F.C., D.S.M., the greatest pioneer solo flyer:

1920   London-Turin-Rome-London. 9½ hours non-stop to Turin. Awarded Britannia Trophy by Royal Aero Club for finest aviation feat in British Empire in 1920.

1921   Sydney-Bundaberg (Queensland), non-stop.

1927   London-Riga.

1928   England-Australia, 11,450 miles in 16 days; 129 hours flying time. First solo flight to Australia.

1931   New York-Natal (Brazil)-Gambia (West Africa)-Casablanca-Madrid-London. First solo flight across South Atlantic; first west to east crossing of South Atlantic; and first Trans-Atlantic flight in a light plane.

1933   London, *en route* Australia, crashed Italian Apennines, January 1933.

Chief flights of Air Commodore Sir Charles Kingsford Smith, M.C., A.F.C., world's greatest pioneer airman:

1915-19   Enlisted First A.I.F.; selected for training Royal Flying Corps.

1921   One of first six pilots of West Australian Airways.

1927   Round Australia with C. T. P. Ulm in a Bristol tourer in 10 days 5¾ hours.

1928   First flight across Pacific Ocean; Oakland (California)-Hawaii-Fiji-Brisbane, 83 hours 11 min. In *Southern Cross* with Ulm, and Harry Lyons and Jim Warner (Americans).

1928   First non-stop flight across Australia, from Point Cook (Victoria) to Perth (W.A.). In *Southern Cross* with Ulm, Litchfield and McWilliams (New Zealander).

1928   First flight across the Tasman Sea, from Richmond, N.S.W. to Christchurch, New Zealand, 14 hours 25 min. In the *Southern Cross* with Ulm, Litchfield and McWilliams.

1930   First successful east-west crossing of the Atlantic Ocean; Ireland-Newfoundland-New York, 31½ hours to Newfoundland. In the *Southern Cross* with Van Dyke, Stannage and Saul; then from New York to California, completing the first journey of an aeroplane around the world, crossing the Equator twice.

1930   Solo flight from England to Australia, 9 days 22¼ hours. In the *Southern Cross Junior.*

1931   Established passenger service, Brisbane, Sydney, Melbourne, Hobart.
With G. U. (Scotty) Allan, in the *Southern Cross*, linked with British aircraft at Akyab to establish first England-Australia airmail.
Loss of *Southern Cloud*. Kingsford Smith reduced to "barn-storming" in the *Southern Cross.*
Attempt to break solo record to London in *Southern Cross Minor* defeated by carbon monoxide poisoning. Following grounding of Allan in the *Southern Sun*, he succeeded in getting 45,288 Christmas airmail letters to London in the *Southern Star.*

1933-34   Flights to New Zealand with P. G. Taylor.

1933   Seven-day record flight Australia-England in Percival Gull.

1934   First west-east crossing of Pacific Ocean; Brisbane-Fiji-Hawaii-Oakland (California). In the *Lady Southern Cross*, a single-engine Lockheed Altair, with P. G. Taylor.

1935   Attempt to fly Jubilee Mail to New Zealand, 4th May. The *Southern Cross's* last great flight.

1935   Record flight, London-Allahabad in 30 hours. In *Lady Southern Cross* with J. T. Pethybridge. Perished off Burma, 7th November.

Pioneer Record of Captain Sir P. G. Taylor, G.C., M.C., greatest trail blazer of the oceans:

1917   Fighter pilot and leader, flying single-seater Sopwith Scout, France. Awarded M.C. for "exceptional dash and gallantry in attacking large formations of hostile aircraft".

1924   First post-war flight Melbourne-Sydney; in DH6 aircraft.

1928   Pioneered astronomical navigation in the air. Designed and used own sextant and other instruments on transocean flights. First civil pilot to hold first class air navigator's licence.

1930   Airline captain on first Australian National Airways services; the first airline to operate instrument flight in all weathers, without radio aids.

1933   Navigator of *Southern Cross* on crossing of Tasman Sea; Gerringong Beach (N.S.W.) to New Plymouth (N.Z.), January. Return flight, Ninety Mile Beach to Sydney.

1933   Navigator and co-pilot, Ulm's *Faith in Australia*, record flight; 6 days, 17 hours; aircraft cruising at 80 knots.

1934   Navigator of *Southern Cross* on experimental transTasman flight, Richmond to New Plymouth; and on return flight, Ninety Mile Beach-Lord Howe Island-Sydney.

1934   Solo record, Batavia-Sydney; in Percival Gull VH-CKS, carrying special films.

1934   Navigator of Lockheed Altair single-engined *Lady Southern Cross* on Kingsford Smith's first west-east crossing of Pacific Ocean.

1935   Navigator of *Southern Cross* on attempted Jubilee Mail flight to New Zealand (pioneer airmail to celebrate Jubilee of King George V and Queen Mary). Awarded Empire Gallantry Medal for repeatedly climbing to outboard engines to transfer oil from damaged to good engine. Subsequently awarded George Cross, in 1942, to replace E.G.M.

1937   Batavia-Sydney record in Percival Gull VH-UVA to deliver pictures of coronation of King George VI.

1939   Leader of first air crossing of Indian Ocean. In P.B.Y. (Catalina) flying boat *Guba*, flew to Port Hedland (W.A.) via Cocos, Diego Garcia and Seychelles Islands to Mombasa (Kenya) Africa; survey of air bases later used by Royal Navy and Royal Air Force for operations in Indian Ocean.

1941   Navigator of Catalina flying boats for R.A.A.F. on delivery flights, Honolulu-Sydney. Record flight, Canton Island-Sydney, non-stop. First airmail Fiji-Sydney.

1942   Commissioned by Royal Netherlands Indies Airways to make special wartime flights to U.S.A. in Royal N.E.I. Navy Catalina, taking Lieut-Governor Dr van Mook, General van Oyen and senior Dutch officials, at time of Japanese invasion of Netherlands East Indies.

1943   Aircraft captain with R.A.F. 45 Atlantic Transport Group; flying aircraft built in North America across Atlantic to United Kingdom.

1944   First crossing of Central Pacific Ocean, Mexico to Australia. Captain of the Catalina *Frigate Bird* on R.A.F. exploratory survey flight of route from U.K. via Bermuda, Nassau, British Honduras, Acapulco (Mexico), Clipperton Island, Tahiti, and other islands of French Polynesia, Cook Islands, Tonga, Auckland, Sydney. Return to Bermuda via Fanning and North Pacific islands. Carried first airmail from Fanning Island.

1945   Captain of RY3 Liberator Privateer, Express Transport, on first British trans-Pacific air service: R.A.F. Transport Command service, San Diego to Sydney, via Honolulu, Canton Island, Nandi (Fiji) and Auckland.

1950   Aircraft captain with Trans-Oceanic Airways on pioneer services, eastern Australia and South-West Pacific.

1951   Captain of Catalina, *Frigate Bird II* on first crossing of South Pacific Ocean, Sydney to South America and return; via Tahiti, Mangareva and Easter Island to Quinteros (near Valparaiso). Awarded Order of Bernado O'Higgins (Liberator of Chile), Grade Commendator, by President Gonzales Videla for services in linking Chile and Australia across Pacific. Carried first official airmail from Australia to South America.

1954   Knighted by Queen Elizabeth II for services as pioneer aviator.

1955   Inaugurated world's first flying boat cruise service, in South Pacific, and flew as captain of his Bermuda flying boat, *Frigate Bird III*, on this service.

EDITOR'S NOTES

MOST BOOKS about the Australian Trail Blazers of the Air have been published only in Australia, and in small editions, so that readers in other countries may have difficulty in finding copies.

A compact *History of Australian Aviation* by Stanley Brogden, with excellent photographs of early aircraft, was published by the Hawthorn Press, Melbourne in 1960. *The Aeronautical Work of Lawrence Hargrave* by T. C. Roughley (Technological Museum, Sydney) contains fascinating diagrams and photographs of Hargrave's box-kites and rotary motors. Volume VIII of the *Official History of Australia in the War of 1914-18* by F. M. Cutlack (Angus and Robertson, Sydney) is a most readable account of the early days of training at Point Cook and of the feats of the Australian Flying Corps in Mesopotamia, Palestine and France. The book has a photograph of the First Half-Flight before they were issued with uniforms.

Sir Thomas White wrote an amusing description of his training at Point Cook and of the early attacks on the Turks by the First Half-Flight. The title of his book, *Guests of the Unspeakable* (Hamilton, London, 1928) means that it is chiefly about the experiences of prisoners-of-war with the Turks and of their attempts to escape. There is a remarkable chapter on the determined Lieutenant Hill (later almost to beat Kingsford Smith on one of his record flights) who feigned madness for many months. Hill, sick with dysentery and with a long, untidy beard, three times a day, for the benefit of the Turks, "completed all the gymnastic postures of the Mohammedan *namaz*, repeating meanwhile in a doleful voice the ritual of the Church of England".

The Bert Hinkler Story is the sub-title of *Solo* by R. D. Mackenzie (Jacaranda Press, Brisbane, 1960). *My Flying Life* is "An authentic biography prepared under the personal supervision of and from the diaries of the late Sir Charles Kingsford Smith, with a Preface by Geoffrey Rawson" (Andrew Melrose, London, 1937).

The most easily procurable of Sir Gordon Taylor's books is *The Sky Beyond* (Cassell, 1963), an exciting story of his flying life from 1916 to 1951. *Pacific Flight* (Angus and Robertson, 1935) is an account of the west-east crossing. *Call to the Winds* (Angus and Robertson, 1939) tells of the *Southern Cross's* last flight over the Tasman. *Forgotten Island* (Shakespeare Head, 1948) is a story of the Clipperton Island survey of the Central Pacific; and *Frigate Bird* (Angus and Robertson, 1954) tells of the long flight across the Pacific to Chile. *Bird of the Islands*, 1964, is the story of his flying boat cruise service in the South Pacific.

The Wandering Years by Arthur H. Affleck (Longmans, 1964) has original material not found elsewhere. *The Dangerous Skies* (Cassell, 1954) by A. E. Clouston gives his account of record-breaking flights. *Flying Matilda* by Norman Ellison (Angus and Robertson, 1957) has many lively anecdotes and fine photographs. Other readable books include *Wings Across the Tasman* by Leslie Jillett (Angus and Robertson, 1953) and Nancy Bird's *Born to Fly* (Angus and Robertson, 1961).

Australian Aviation, A Bibliography, compiled by the Public Library of Victoria, is a most helpful guide to anyone searching through the early flying magazines.

At the Sydney Museum of Applied Arts and Sciences may be seen monoplane models made by Lawrence Hargrave and one of his box-kites. One of the Deperdussins used at Central Flying School, 1914 is housed in the R.A.A.F. Museum at Point Cook. The Vickers-Vimy in which Sir Ross and Sir Keith Smith made the first flight from England to Australia is preserved at the Adelaide Aerodrome. Their maps are in the Mitchell Library, Sydney.

The Avro Avian in which Bert Hinkler flew solo from London to Riga and later to Australia is now in the Brisbane Museum.

Brisbane Airpoint was the scene of two of Kingsford Smith's greatest triumphs. Brisbane was the city of his birth. There, now carefully preserved in "The Kingsford Smith National Memorial", erected with money subscribed by the people, is the *Southern Cross*, the aeroplane which blazed more air routes than any other, "The Father of the Fokkers". In the opinion of the Department of Civil Aviation, to whose courtesy the author is indebted, the *Southern Cross* is the property of the Australian people.

The author acknowledges a debt to Sir Patrick Gordon Taylor who so courteously read this book in manuscript; and to Professor C. Day Lewis and his publishers, Jonathan Cape, for permission to quote four stanzas from the symphonic poem "A Time to Dance". The whole of this stirring poem may be read in *Collected Poems, 1935*.

In a small book of his verse, *Sky Saga* (Hutchinson), given to the author and valued by her, the late Sir Thomas White wrote these lines:

> A wealth of selflessness has found expression here,
> Where each knew the risk, how short the span might be,
> Yet did not falter.

K.T.

Lawrence Hargrave

Bert Hinkler

Raymond Parer & J.C. McIntosh